HOW YOU FEED A CAT

(That Is, How You Feed a Cat Because I Told You to
Feed the Cat and You Listened to Me)

Edward H. West, MD

ISBN 979-8-88751-023-1 (paperback)
ISBN 979-8-88751-024-8 (digital)

Christian Faith Publishing
832 Park Avenue
Meadville, PA 16335
www.christianfaithpublishing.com

All scripture quotations, unless otherwise indicated, are taken from the New American Standard Bible, © 1960, 1962, 1963, 1968, 1971, 1972, 1973, 1975, 1977, 1995 by The Lockman Foundation. Used by permission.

Scripture quotations indicated as ESV are taken from The Holy Bible, English Standard Version, Copyright © 2016 by Crossway Bibles, a division of Good News Publishers. Used by permission. All rights reserved.

Scripture quotations indicated as NKJV are taken from the New King James Version. Copyright © 1979, 1980, 1982 by Thomas Nelson, Inc. Used by permission. All rights reserved.

Printed in the United States of America

Contents

Part 1: A Parent under Construction

Part One is my personal story. It tells how I learned the secrets of resolving the issues of children who do not "listen" and effectively converting "bad attitudes." It also tells how I changed for the better and came closer to being the father God intended me to be.

Part 2: Coming to Terms with Child-rearing

Part Two is a clarification of definitions of words used by parents—words like "listening," "obedience," and "respect." There is much to learn just by considering the meaning of these words. When the specific definitions are always applied, it is easier to see solutions.

Part 3: Making Disciples in the Home

Part Three considers the paradox that your child is always learning but is not necessarily teachable—at least, by you. Learning to spot your child's teachable moments can be transforming in your relationship and in your success as his first, and most important, teacher.

Part 4: How You Feed a Cat

Part Four confronts the sad truth that frustration in childrearing is partially explained by parental flaws and misfirings. With hope, it also considers biblical solutions for us.

Introduction

My first editor thought that the title of this book—*How You Feed a Cat*—should be changed. He said parents would only find this book on practical, biblical child-rearing in the pets section of the bookstore. But the title describes the essence of my subject.

This book is not about how *to* feed a cat. That would be spectacularly tedious and not worth reading. Rather, it is about how *you*, as a parent, give your child a direction, and he simply complies promptly, efficiently, and cheerfully the first time you give the direction. It is about how *you*, my child, feed the cat *because* I told you to do so.

In a large view, child-rearing is about you learning and practicing an effective role in your child's process of change. Your child is inevitably moving toward maturity and much of the process occurs regardless of your efforts. The challenge for you is to fulfill your limited role well, and here's the truth:

You *cannot control* the outcome.

You *can influence* the self-esteem and self-control of your child.

You *can control* your own change and become a more effective parent.

The book has four parts, introduced by stories from my life as a pediatrician and a father. The remaining parts shed light on how you get your child to feed the cat by applying biblical wisdom.

My personal stories usually involve my own two daughters, along with boys and girls I have known. In referring generally to parents and their children, I use masculine pronouns for simplicity. I ask that you forgive the pronouns if this is a problem.

Finally, in case you doubt that you *can* feed a cat simply because your child listened and did it, consider the answer from our Lord to a doubting parent: "And Jesus said to him, 'If you *can*? All things are possible to him who believes!'" (Mark 9:23).

How You Don't Get the Dishes Done

During a routine office visit with an eleven-year-old boy, his mother asked me, "How do you make your kid do the dishes?"

Do the dishes? My mother trained me how to do the dishes when I was younger than the kid sitting across from me. She also stayed with me at the sink to make sure I was doing them right. Then at night, she stayed with me as I prayed the way she had taught me: "Help me to be a good boy, to mind Mommy, and to love Jesus."

By the time I was eleven, I was a reliable dishwasher whose policy was to wash the dishes whenever required. So I knew all about the subject. But because I was now the child's doctor, I suppressed my little boy inside and replied, "Really? Tell me why you ask."

She then told me how you *don't* get the dishes done. "Well, his one chore in our home is to do the supper dishes. After supper, I remind him, and he mutters that he'll get to it after a while. So I say, 'Now!' and he tells me to stop bugging him. Then his father says, 'Do what your mother says,' and then threatens him. My son blows him off, and my husband gets mad and leaves. The dishes eventually get done, but not very well, and every night it's the same battle."

I checked with the office nurse to see if I had the time for a conversation, then sat back to discuss the subject of kids washing dishes. I spoke of establishing effective authority, listening, attitude, reputation, and discipline as training, not noise. I told her that we tend to be task oriented with our children rather than coming alongside them as coaches and training them to obey consistently and perform well by practices. I pointed out that the practice he was receiving was in arguing and procrastination. He was also practicing *not* washing the dishes.

I then raised the idea that she may be working with an imaginary child who gets the dishes done when she says so. But she is actually engaging her real boy, a famous non-dishwasher, for the task. I then told a story to illustrate how to bring a halt to the futile nightly encounters and return to a normal conversation, peaceful digestion, and clean dishes.

My daughter was eleven years old when one day, her mother told her to feed the cat. My wife was at the sink, washing dishes; Julie was sitting at the kitchen counter reading a magazine, and I was sitting at the table with a book. The cat was meowing around on the floor.

My wife said, "Julie, please feed the cat."

Julie kept reading, and the cat kept meowing. After a minute or two, my wife said again, "Julie, please feed the cat."

Nothing. The cat kept meowing, and I thought, *She should have told me to feed the cat. If she had, the cat would have been fed the first time.*

Then I awakened to the fact that war had just been declared, and I had a responsibility. Her mother and I were always committed allies in a contest with Julie. In those days, a periodic dustup with Julie was part of life. She was inclined to reject the idea that her parents were in charge even when she had been too young to have the thought.

Through the years, I had learned that I couldn't simply give Julie a direction and expect obedience. There was something about her mood of the moment that would render her either compliant or resistant, and I had developed a skill in figuring out these moments. Yet after a decade of experiences, periodically she would still resist an imposition on her will. So once again, I would go off to war—peaceably, of course.

From six feet away, I clapped my book closed and locked my eyes on hers. Quietly, like a sheriff in a dusty cow town street calling out a mean *hombre*, I said, "Julie, feed the cat!"

She cut her eyes toward me in a momentary glare, slammed her magazine down, stomped to the closet, grabbed the bag of dry cat food and the empty bowl, poured some of the kibbles into the bowl (and some onto the floor), unceremoniously stuffed the bag away, and then slammed the bowl down. Stomping back to her seat, she closed the scene by dramatically wedging the magazine directly in front of her face.

There followed a moment of silence—like the silence in heaven before the final bowl of wrath is poured out in the Apocalypse.

I arose, retrieved the cat food bag, and poured the contents of the bowl back into the bag. I quietly set the empty bowl on the floor and the bag back in the closet, then calmly sat down. "Julie," I purred. "That's not how you feed cats."

These two unfinished stories about how you get children to wash dishes and feed cats are the inspiration for this book. When children are involved, dishes don't get washed, and cats don't get fed for many reasons. Some children have hearing or communication problems, some have problems with self-control, and some are physically, emotionally, developmentally, or intellectually incapable. These kids may fail because of limitations that are not their fault.

Some dishes don't get washed, and some cats don't get fed because the children told to do so have not been trained to wash dishes or to feed cats. They fail because they are uninformed and unskilled. Other children fail because they have had too many practices in doing it wrong; they have actually developed proficiency in failure. Finally, failure continues because they just give up and develop a bad attitude.

In these sad, futile repetitions, meanwhile, their parents seem unaware that they are commanding imaginary children to obey. The real ones in front of them have largely learned how not to do the tasks because of the ineffective commands and are becoming more skilled at maintaining a bad attitude. Whatever the original reason may be that a child does not simply obey a parent's direction, there is usually a final, common pathway: "I don't feed the cat because I *will not* feed the cat." This policy of deliberate resistance then becomes a hard shell that closes down the joy of being a parent. The crisis moment with Julie was based on this. She had set her will to dominate the will of her parents.

Everyone knows how to feed a cat. How to feed a cat is not the issue. The issue is how I get *you*, my child, to feed a cat because I say it, and you do it.

Nobody really likes being told what to do; some people *really* don't like it. This is why some people prefer a jail cell or a homeless shelter or a desert island to submitting to authority. People can be this way with teachers, bosses, and the government. Some are this way with God.

It seems that certain children distinguish themselves as bomb throwers very early in life. These specimens rehearse a script with their parents in a mystery soap opera that plays each day in the home. The script is practiced by parents who know that when they tell their child to wash a dish or feed a cat, it will not happen. But they tell them again anyway.

It is not the outcome that is a mystery. The mystery is why this script continues. The mystery drama is not particularly entertaining or enjoyable, and it seems that it would get old. If mysteries like these play in your life regularly, keep reading.

PART 1

A Parent under Construction

"ABOUT...FACE!"

When I was a child, I used to speak like a child,
think like a child, reason like a child; when I became
a man, I did away with childish things.

—*1 Corinthians 13:11*

Becoming a Children's Doctor

In the fall of 1964, I was facing physics and organic chemistry as a junior in college. Meanwhile, my parents and two younger brothers were in a State Department orientation program for families moving to South Vietnam. The military situation overseas fell apart that winter, so my family stayed home, and my father moved alone to Saigon as a civilian government agent.

I did well with academics that year, and when Dad came home for a brief respite, he asked about my plans after graduation the following spring. I would go to Vietnam in the army, I supposed. That was what everyone else I knew was doing. He asked why I didn't apply to medical school. I told him that I didn't know why. So I did. And a few weeks later, I received an acceptance letter.

This little moment of critical guidance from my father was not common. As the days of my childhood passed, it usually seemed that I was making up my own story. I was one of four boys along for the ride in my family, contributing to the general project of a happy home. My parents were totally devoted to each other, and they enjoyed our life together. They never seemed overly impressed when I did well, and when I made a mess, they were not outwardly stressed. But they did expect me to confess, clean up the mess, make amends, take whatever medicine I had coming, and then start again.

In the trusting atmosphere of my home, I learned both liberty and responsibility. My parents were my confidants, providers, and protectors but not my overseers or bosses. Yet, they were always in charge. When I was young, Dad clarified his status by reminding me, "I am your father, not your friend." He did not often tell me what to do, but when he did, it was my policy to listen to him.

My earliest memory of my dad acting like a father was in a moment of my indifference to my mother's call to come to supper. (I must have been about three years old.) I was dawdling on the stairs when a giant whirlwind swept me up with an iron grip and unceremoniously dumped me in my room. That tornado was my father, supporting my mother's authority. I don't remember the outcome, but it must have been satisfactory because I don't remember experiencing the whirlwind again.

I was born as my father's submarine was entering enemy waters on a Pacific war patrol. In my early years, his navy duties kept him busy; my mother was my primary caregiver. She was a sunny, casual, former schoolteacher who could keep me and my brothers in line by a distinctive sound noticed by no one but the West boys.

On more than one Sunday in our large downtown Charleston church, she would interrupt the quietness of the sanctuary by clearing her throat—"*Ahem*"—when I was fooling around in the balcony with some of my reprobate friends. This primordial call meant the bell had ended recess. I would remain in order until the benediction.

My father was awarded the Silver Star for valor after the war. I only knew this because I asked about a clipped newspaper article I found in a family scrapbook. He otherwise never spoke about this award. Neither did he speak to me about the divorce of his parents when he was a young teenager or about his sister's taking her own life as a young woman. I knew almost nothing about his side of our family because his conversation was focused on the wonders of my mother's family, reserving special praise for her. In my imagination and with a little help from Hollywood, I concluded that World War II was won, thanks to my dad and John Wayne.

My four years of college were spent as a cadet at The Citadel. The commandant assured my parents that he would tenderly complete the work in me that they had begun. As a freshman, I quickly learned to fully submit to authority without apparent resistance. I practiced responding to commands promptly and efficiently. Upperclassmen would search the deepest recesses of my brain, looking for my attitude, but whatever resistance they were seeking, they never found. They were in charge, and I was okay with that.

I never really felt at ease at The Citadel; there was always ten-sion, brought on by the presence of authority. It seemed as though I was a combat reporter on the edge of danger, observing and trying to make sense of something that didn't make much sense. The four years changed me, though. I entered as a clueless teenager. I gradu-ated as an adult with a policy of self-inspection and paying attention. I am grateful for that.

When I began my medical education, my father was still a State Department officer in the steamy Vietnamese boonies, advising vil-lage councilmen who were trying to make local democracy work as they ducked bombs and bullets. For a month of terror during the Tet Offensive, Dad was an unarmed civilian, hunkered down in his little apartment in the suburbs of Hue. He never spoke of this in any detail to me, just as he never spoke of passing under the minefields into the Sea of Japan in 1945.

After his death in 1989, I learned that the reason he volunteered for service in Vietnam was to earn hazardous duty extra pay. He used that income to pay the cost of my medical education. I also learned that he had symptoms of PTSD at home in his retirement years. I don't remember my father ever telling me directly that he loved me, and he never spoke to me about any of these things. It was my youngest brother who told me about Dad's ordeal when he returned and of his intentions and kindness toward me. Dad is long gone now, but in all the years that passed, I never doubted his love.

I believed when I was accepted at medical school that I would surely one day be a doctor. I also knew that the only kind of doctor I wanted to be was a pediatrician. Scientific information in the first two years of school blew into my face like water from a fire hose. A fair amount was learned just by coming to understand the meaning of the multisyllabic terms of medical jargon. If I knew that *dermis* was skin and that *epi* was above, I knew what *epidermis* was without being told. Accurate communication is vital to medical understand-ing, so I learned to use the words precisely.

There were many times that I would receive back my graded examination paper and be grateful that I had passed, even though I no longer recognized the information I had apparently mastered several weeks earlier. Sometimes, I didn't even remember studying the material, much less remember the answers. But I kept on passing and learning.

My most distinct memory of medical school was the day I was handed a diploma and shook hands with someone important. My thought was, *Yesterday I was a student, today I am a doctor—and I am no smarter today than I was yesterday.* I walked across the stage with a grim, new purpose not to fail the children who would be counting on me.

Becoming a Daddy

After a year of medical education, I married Gwen, my best friend from high school. In those times, evenings for us were simple. I studied while she graded the history tests of her eighth graders at the local laundromat. We learned loyalty and endurance as we accepted the solitude of our evenings.

Gwen's mother was an only child with some disturbing childhood memories. She was attentive to her two daughters and always maintained a kind conversation when I was around. She was a very proper lady. When I asked to marry her daughter, she was a little skeptical about the prospect of a son-in-law without a salary. But she was tolerant and invariably gracious to me.

Gwen's father was a big quiet man who had never known his father. He had emigrated alone from Scotland when he was a wee lad. When I knew him, he was a church elder with high standards. I knew he had a temper; it came out occasionally when he was driving Gwen and me somewhere. (She and I usually had no car otherwise.) He seemed to really enjoy my company and was all in favor of my proposal for his daughter.

In spite of their bumpy childhoods, these two parents had turned out a remarkable young woman for me to marry. Gwen was an earnest student with an academic record better than mine. She also had higher standards and expectations than I did. I knew that she would improve me in a marriage because she would not let me drag her down to my level. I am not sure how she coped with medical school because I was gone so much, but she was always there when I got home.

A number of my classmates in medical school were married. Gwen and I had a modest social life with some of these couples, but we were usually too busy, too tired, or too broke to participate. Gwen didn't complain. She accepted my absence and developed her own life of private devotions and meditation that strengthened her.

In the first months after graduation, we were stunned by the number of married couples who had endured medical school with us but were now divorcing. Many of these new doctors were finding replacement wives among the young nurses and medical techs who had been their companions during long hospital nights on call. This was sobering for the two of us, and I came to appreciate the character and grit of my wife even more.

I was an intern in pediatrics when I received a letter from the US Selective Service. Beginning with "Greeting," my draft board cheerfully told me that as soon as my internship was over that year, I would be in the army, either as a doctor or a grunt. If I chose to be a physician, I would not be drafted; I would be a compulsory volunteer. So I volunteered.

Gwen was expecting in 1971 when I was fitted for my captain's uniform. The Vietnam War was winding down, but I assumed I would be "leaving on a jet plane" for that place, as Peter, Paul, and Mary used to sing. Instead, a few months later, I was practicing in a small army clinic in Virginia.

I had spent the first year after graduation listening for heart murmurs and learning how to put the point of a tiny needle into a tiny channel of a baby's vertebra to tap spinal fluid. In the army, I was a general medical officer, dealing with everything from emergency trauma to sunburn. Meanwhile, Gwen delivered on Christmas Day.

I was surprised at how I instantly attached to my baby Alice and at how much joy she gave me simply by being in my life. After a few months, I would amuse her with silly stuff, and she would squeal and giggle, and then she was imitating what she saw and heard. I had passed examinations on the developmental milestones of children and understood the science. But to actually see her reach points of social and motor skills fascinated me.

Alice may not have been intentionally working on our relationship in those days, but she clearly came to know me as her buddy. Her first word around nine months was *Da-Da*. Before she was a year old, we were sharing sips of a lime-green, citrus soft drink. Her second word was "Dew."

Life in the army was like opening wide all the big windows of a stuffy room. My professional work was usually not stressful, although many of my patients were freshly home from the war and undergoing complex adjustments along with their families. This was when I first found personal fulfillment in family counseling. I was also learning the depth of dark secrets in families and alternative ways people can experience marriage and family.

At home, the three of us had time to bond and work on the routine issues that popped up between family members. I have no memory of Alice resisting my authority when she was a toddler, although she must have occasionally. I taught her without the conscious thought that I was her teacher. I wasn't smart enough to seek wisdom about being a father. I must have assumed that her mother and I would figure out how to rear Alice.

I now realize that I was raising my child the way I was raised. I was taught to trust the Bible as truthful when I was young; then in college, I added the truth of science. I even learned to combine the ideas of psychological experts with divine truth. But if I had been wiser, I would have noticed that my personal experiences and the correct answers on psychology exams sometimes did not match biblical principles. If all of these sources for child-rearing were true, they would not have been contradictory.

When I was young, I had processed certain scriptures pertaining to children as a child. But I did not consider their implications for me as an adult and parent. For instance, I knew as a child that the fifth commandment, "Honor your father and your mother, that your days may be prolonged in the land the Lord your God has given you" (Exodus 20:12), was to be taught repeatedly to the Hebrew children. I assumed then that the divine order applied to children.

But the Ten Commandments were delivered to the adults of Israel when Moses came down from Mount Sinai. The fifth commandment, like the others, was for me as an adult now. The biblical concept of teaching a child to honor his parents arises from the Hebrew word *kabed*, which translates to *honor*. The intention of the commandment is that a child should be taught a profound insight into his parent's worth and then practice responding well to the parent according to that insight. Such insight is a function of years of interactions and shared experiences. It requires the parent's investment of quality time into the relationship, along with frequent, memorable conversations.

I believed that the Bible was correct and that honor was the foundation of the parent-child relationship. But I did not consider that if my little one ever honored me, it would be the result of my teaching her about the parents who cherished her in the context of a reliable, committed fellowship. In this state of ignorance as a parent, I completed my military obligation and entered pediatric residency in Atlanta. That's where a crisis in my relationship with twenty-month-old Alice brought insight to me, then changed me. Just being a daddy would not be enough.

Becoming a Father

Alice had grown used to my being home and having lots of fun times when I was an army doctor. But in residency, I left our little apartment before she was awake and did not return until her bedtime. Every third night, I worked at the hospital through the night and would be so tired the following evening that I was commonly asleep on the sofa before supper. On our occasional encounters at home, it became apparent that our relationship had changed. She was still usually obedient, but she no longer came to me or spontaneously talked with me. It must have seemed by my absence that I had dumped her, and she could no longer rely on me as a companion.

That's when I first considered that adults with life experiences and capacities might accept solitude and even come to appreciate it, but a little kid just can't endure separation and boredom. Alice was doing the best she could with my absence, but I could do more to help. I needed to step up to the work of being a father.

My plan was simple. I knew that when three-year-olds are together, they normally interact in play, while two-year-olds in similar circumstances play in parallel. They seem unaware of the presence of the others except when they are simultaneously going for the same toy. Toddlers normally develop social awareness and enjoy mutual play some months after their second birthday. I was the big boy, so I changed for the sake of my little girl.

When I was home on weekends, I would sit in the room where Alice was playing by herself and observe what she was doing in play. Then I would do what she was doing a few feet away, without looking at her or talking. When she was sitting on the floor, rolling a ball, I would be on the floor with another ball. When she was dressing a doll at a table, I would be nearby at a table with my own doll (!).

With the passage of a little time, Alice went from glancing my way to moving nearer. Before long, she was rolling a ball to me or exchanging an article of doll clothing; occasionally, we might even speak a little. Soon we were back on track as buddies. When I was available on a summer evening, we would be in the parking lot, catching lightning bugs until bedtime. Then I would sing her songs while she was in the tub and read her stories until night-night. The results of adult decisions had been forced into her little life, and she had matured to the point of accepting and adapting to the new reality of my absence and unreliability.

Just before her third birthday, Alice's solitary role was challenged by a new baby sister, Julie. In Julie's first year or so, I was the *absent parent* once again, only this time, it was with a baby who had not first gotten to know me the way Alice had. Julie primarily bonded with her mother who was *always there.*

I had learned the importance of bonding from Alice, so when I could be with Julie, I concentrated on our relationship. The result was that I shamelessly enjoyed her as she grew through infancy. I consciously did not give commands or directions to Julie in those days, although at the time, I didn't know the wisdom of indulging an immature princess in the days before she was old enough to practice being contrary.

In her first months, there was no need to tell her what to do because she was too young to perceive authority. She was also without language insight and without willful self-control. She did love to be loved though, and I loved to love her. So that was our relationship—all fellowship, no authority.

As months passed and she became a toddler, I gratefully found that those moments we had enjoyed together were golden. Later, when she defiantly closed down our wonderful bond behind a door she slammed shut, the stress and mounting pressure of self-imposed isolation always led her to repentance and return. Spoiling her as a baby had paid dividends as an incentive to come out of her room and sincerely reconcile with me.

Meanwhile, Alice noticed my obvious attention to her sister when I was home, and she naturally wondered about it. She soon learned that if she *bothered* the baby in play, Gwen or I would inter-vene and speak to her about proper manners in words she probably did not understand but enjoyed hearing. From Alice's perspective, she had been the focus of our conversation before the baby showed up. Now the baby had replaced her, and she had learned that by bothering the baby, she was back in the saddle for our conversation.

The issue of Alice deliberately disrupting Julie's tranquility grew. *Somebody had to do something.* For the sake of the children, it was time for a father to step in.

I was still only home occasionally, and Gwen was stretched between the two children. Carping at Alice when she was on the prowl for the baby (which was typically when our attention was else-where) only promoted the problem. By ineffectively complaining, we were unintentionally stimulating her and steering her into a habit of bothering her sister. The problem needed to be fixed decisively, and my time at home was limited. So when the moment was convenient, and Alice was rested and in a good mood, our conversation went something like this:

"Alice, you like to bother the baby."

No response.

"I want to teach you not to do that."

Still nothing.

I got down on my hands and knees on the floor where she was playing and aggressively placed my face within an inch or two of her face. She was surprised and moved away to reestablish her space. I moved with her and kept my face engaged. She moved again and so did I. Then she began to cry (which broke my heart.) I comforted her in our familiar snuggle and said, "Honey, that's how Julie feels when you bother her. Do you understand?"

She nodded, and I held her and told her she must learn to leave her sister alone. She understood—and it *worked!* It also helped that Gwen and I developed a new practice of conversation with the girls. Both girls benefited from our voices, but because of their ages, only Alice could make some sense of what we were saying. So when we were tending to Julie and Alice was present, we practiced directing our conversation toward Alice.

In my dreams, I wanted my little girls to love each other. But I had not considered what the process of learning to love your sister might look like. *Love* expresses positive virtues such as kindness and patience. But for young children in their first relationship of equal status (the sibling relationship), the first teaching of love is that they must learn not to bother each other. Paul wrote about this negative of love in his letters: "Love does no wrong to a neighbor; therefore love is the fulfillment of the law" (Romans 13:10). Before I could teach them to be kind to each other, I would first have to teach them not to harass each other.

Teaching Alice was usually easy because she was so compliant and willing to learn. By age four, we were consistently enjoying some important conversations arising from bedtime stories. Also, she learned from popular music that Daddy loved her "like a rock," and she was secure in that. It took a while for me to see that Alice was teachable in a way that Julie was not and that this had to do with her consistent acceptance of my authority. I was one father with two very different children. I would have to adjust to this reality.

Becoming a Partner

I completed residency in 1975. We moved to Charleston, and I began a career in general pediatrics, working in several hospitals, separated by twenty miles. Meanwhile, nine-month-old Julie had revealed her royal entitlement by routinely resisting our direction. One of her first words that autumn was "No!"

Before long, I realized that I had taught her to say "No!" even though we probably did not have the same idea in mind when we used the word. I would sharply say it when I intended for her to stop and stay stopped. She would sharply say "No!" when she was about to go her own way, and I was standing athwart. Either way, we weren't communicating our ideas very well, and her defiance was increasing because I was unintentionally giving her practices in defiance.

So Gwen and I deliberately changed how we dealt with her. For instance, we saw that Julie was likely to be uncooperative when she needed a nap or was in a stressful moment of confusion. But there were also times she would cooperate (often for reasons unknown.) We became more accurate in figuring out those times.

We learned that we if could judge her mood before speaking to her, we could improve her cooperation and reduce the noise. So according to Julie's moment, we spoke or remained silent as we worked around her and accomplished our purposes. We also subtly corrected each other when one of us was flummoxed by Julie, but the other wasn't directly involved.

Our basic policy was not to give her directions or commands unless she was in an obedient moment because each ineffective command actually produced another practice in defiance. When we had things to get done and she was part of the project, we would usually not speak our intentions and not tell her what to do. We would merely remain silent and bring her along as we accomplished the objective because getting things done was not necessarily the same as rearing children. For example, we might not mention that it was suppertime, but in a moment, she would simply find that she was sitting in her restraining chair at the table. This policy of reticence seemed to help until the State Department of Motor Vehicles got involved.

When Julie was a baby, she had been accustomed to being held in Gwen's arms in the front seat of the car. Then in 1976, the state legislature mandated child seat restraints for toddlers. Her resistance to sitting alone in the rear, trapped in a little seat and facing backward, soon threatened to get us in trouble with the highway patrol.

Having some success with our policy of not using commands to get things done and working as partners, Gwen and I discussed a plan and agreed that we would train her into the new reality of her travel restrictions. We would gradually condition her to accept the reversed car seat by only placing her in the car for trips when Gwen could sit in the rear beside her. This seemed to work as long as Gwen was right there with her.

During this time, if Gwen wasn't making the trip, Julie didn't either. As Julie only had successful practices, the back seat drama ended surprisingly quickly. The next milestone was getting Gwen out of the back seat while leaving Julie alone, restrained, unable to see us, yet remain at peace. We began the practices toward this goal only when Julie didn't need a nap, and we had the time. Oh, and especially when we had no place to go.

Julie would only be in the car when we were parked and practicing with her. Gwen would lock her in her little car seat and sit with her for a moment to ensure there was no resistance as I turned on the ignition and idled. Gwen would then shift in the seat as though she were about to get out of the car. Before Julie could react, Gwen would resume her reassuring sitting posture beside the car seat. Julie might momentarily be on the verge of protest, but the action happened so smoothly and rapidly that it was over before she could react. Gwen repeated this until Julie no longer seemed to notice Gwen's shifting toward the door.

Next, Gwen moved and opened the door, closing it before Julie could react. Before long, Julie accepted these actions without seeming to notice, so Gwen began getting out and then quickly back in the car. Finally, she could leave Julie restrained in the back seat, close the door, and sit in the front without any protest from the rear. During all of these moments of practice, Gwen maintained a continuous, reassuring conversation.

Our commitment to patiently help our toddler adjust to change rather than simply forcing change on her was the beginning of a three-way partnership. All of us learned to accept each other as we worked together on our project. We came to see that child-rearing did not have to be a wrestling match. It could be more like a dance, where sometimes the partners are holding on to each other and sometimes dancing apart but in a coordinated manner. In such a dance, someone must be in charge; yet, to an observer, that person of status is not noticeable. When it worked, the partnership brought peace.

In my dealings with Julie and her resistance, I first realized that a parent may assume he has authority, but if the child does not agree and submit, the parent's authority has no impact on behavior. In actually dealing with children, the only parental authority that matters is *effective* authority. Beyond the capacity to command obedience, effective authority actually results in obedience.

Another reality I began to consider was the uniqueness of how authority works in the family. I knew that when authority results in obedience in adult society, it is usually because a credible threat that requires submission is acknowledged. This is the coercive authority of a policeman or a drill sergeant. Coercive authority is effective because the credible threat is likely to inflict consequences.

But authority in the family works differently from authority in society. The cherishing and love in a family and the obligation to learn from each other makes authority in the family less like coercive authority and much more like teaching authority. Teaching authority is not empowered by coercion but rather by humility. A teacher is one who has a lesson to impart and is ready to offer it to one who is willing to receive it.

Family authority is more like dancing than law enforcement or military command. If you watch a couple in a dance, there is an unspoken coordination of their movements, so there must be some direction involved—but it's hard to say who is in charge of the direction. The partners seem to just intuitively take cues and work together.

Most American parents assume they are in charge of their children. But infants initially have no insight into threat. They may react to the pain of a swat or may startle to a loud voice, but they do not have the insight to associate the pain or loud voice with a requirement to obey.

Many older infants (like Julie) may recognize the threat but are not impressed. They disagree that they are not in charge and that they must submit. Meanwhile, parents are limited by law as to how far they can go in coercing the obedience of their children. Coercion may work when the parent has physical and psychological advantages. *But ultimately, coercion is not the answer for parents; dancing is better.*

Child-rearing is like dancing.

Becoming the Father of Sisters

It seemed to me that my young daughters had a relationship like I had with my older brother. It wasn't perfect but generally amicable and without stress. I was the second of four boys and remember that there were periodic disputes among us as we grew up together. We sprouted as pairs into two groups of two; in our respective pairs, we were within two-or-so years of each other. My older brother and I moved through school in the same culture, then a few years later, the younger pair did the same. Typical family photographs show my older brother and me outside in a large tub with a garden hose or side by side in the surf of a Charleston beach.

The only times I can recall my parents dealing with sibling issues was sometimes on very long car trips when boredom led to noise in the back seat. I distinctly remember my father stopping the car and getting out. Then he would open our door, grasp the heads of the two miscreants, and bong them together like coconuts. That impressed me. I don't remember if mine was ever one of the two heads, but my lack of memory may be explained by the event itself.

As preschoolers, my girls had separate bedrooms. By then, I knew that they were different individuals, and I consciously tried to accept them that way. I really did love them as they were and tried to deal with each of them according to their developmental stage and personality, including the reality that Alice was usually teachable and Julie not so much. Sibling issues were not on my radar, however.

I was awakened to the pressure parents felt from sibling rivalry by mothers who frequently requested advice on checkups. Most of these conversations were limited to situational solutions. The mothers were not usually inclined toward a philosophical discussion of the

19

intention of a child's heart (see Genesis 8:20–21). They just wanted the racket upstairs to stop.

Meanwhile, in my own home, my girls would periodically tangle, and I would ineffectively complain like the parents I was counseling. Occasionally I might assert some authority for a temporary cease-fire, the way one might swat away a pesky fly at a summer picnic. Perhaps I lazily justified my attitude with, "They'll figure it out as they grow older."

But one aggravation occurred almost every evening which converted me into a zealot for peaceful sibling relationships. My routine in the evenings was to read with them as they snuggled on my lap. I noticed that during reading times, they would engage in a minor elbowing contest like a pair of thoroughbreds snorting neck and neck in the stretch. I didn't have a favorite in the race, but they both intended to win the best position, and I soon realized that telling them to stop was pointless.

When I considered the adults in my life who still had problems in their relationships with brothers and sisters, I realized that siblings begin their lives clueless about relationships. They first learn by whatever happens between them and their primary caregivers. Then, with no insight into how to live with a peer, they find this person in the home who is like themselves.

So without intentional adult supervision and instruction in getting along, most of what children learn about the sibling relationships is by random trial and error. Usually, one child dominates as the two learn and practice dysfunctional coping skills—arguing, whining, physical aggression, manipulation, cruelty, and victimhood.

Having decided that I would become an advocate for proper family relationships, I came to realize that my home was a laboratory where I could experiment with my young daughters, teaching them to enjoy their relationship as they matured. My girls would be *trained* to get along with each other on my lap.

On the first evening of sister lab, the little ones were at play when I entered the room with one of their favorite books and sat down. They ran over and climbed in my lap, pressing for the best position. When the wrestling match began, I stood up and dumped them to the floor. "If you want to sit on my lap," I said, "you have to leave each other alone." Then I sat down again and they climbed back aboard.

Seconds later, I could feel the tension again. I stood again, saying, "No more reading for now."

This became my committed practice each evening until, before long, they had each learned to tolerate the presence of the other and to share my lap without contention. A properly shared lap was better than no lap.

Soon there was a new sibling crisis. Julie had been exposed to a heresy in the church nursery taught by a religious zealot in pull-ups: a toddler was biting his little fellow believers, including Julie. I became aware of this church scandal after Julie began biting Alice at home. I spoke with the nursery ladies who told me that they were sternly warning the perp and removing him from the crime scene each Sunday. But the spree continued and Julie had learned to bite.

I didn't think that what the church ladies were doing would work because biting is based on a momentary, uncontrolled impulse, and the biter becomes more competent with each bite. I noticed this with Julie. She had become quite proficient in mugging her sister, and my late arrival added to the general chaos. Since arrests and lectures did not stop the assaults, I decided to wait silently, watch for the moment of violence, and learn.

When the two were together, for no apparent reason, a darkness crossed Julie's face; then she lunged toward her sister's arm. Although I couldn't identify the trigger, I realized that I could recognize the moment that the evil thought occurred. Julie was too young for reasoning, and apparently, I only encouraged her when I corrected her after the mistake. So I began teaching Alice survival skills; meanwhile, in silence, I began to physically steer Julie away from a life of crime.

I told Alice that she must learn to watch Julie and not turn her back toward her when they were at play. I also told her that I would try to stay near when they were together to remind her in a secret way until the biting was over. As for Julie and me, she was out of the nursery, and I became a sheepdog watching the flock. When a moment was imminent, I would move swiftly toward Julie without speaking and redirect her with my hand at her shoulder. Julie quickly lost her appetite, and the moment passed. When it returned, I silently headed it off again before she could make a mistake. This became a regular practice whenever I could be on duty.

Toddler biting is a bad habit which is notoriously difficult to break. Separation ends the biting for the moment, but a toddler may not even associate the isolation with the biting. Fussing or *reasoning* with a toddler who cannot yet put two words together certainly doesn't help. Asking Julie why she would bite was a good way to learn nonsense and promote the activity.

Julie was a young toddler when her biting began. She was too young for reasoning but *not* too young for disciplining. In this case, discipline was the nonverbal practice *of only doing it right*. Because my interventions were necessarily sporadic, Julie's biting habit was a sporadic problem for years.

As an older child, Julie would be required to confess and sincerely apologize. If Alice had aggravated the situation, she would have to apologize as well; then both girls would have to apologize to *me* because *nobody* could treat *my* little girl that way—including her sister. A spoken prayer that the Lord would help us not to act crazy and a penalty that worked would be imposed following the apology. During this time, I became certain that *the first commandment of a good sibling relationship is not "Love one another." It is "Leave the other one alone."*

Becoming a Bible Teacher

As far back as I can remember, I have been receptive to teaching. Sometimes in my early schooling, I learned quickly; at other times, especially beyond high school, I was confused. My efforts then would be focused more on memorizing and passing tests than on learning. But regardless, I still practiced the disciplines of a student, figuring out how to move to the next level of understanding.

Some of the first formal teaching I received was in Sunday school, learning Bible stories and memorizing scripture. This instruction in Bible continued through high school, and it was in a youth Bible study that I met the girl I would marry. Attending Sunday services was a routine part of our married life, frequently interrupted by the demands of medical training and later, medical practice. In Charleston, I became a Bible teacher, and this began to change my life.

One of the first principles I learned about Bible teaching was that I had to learn beyond my class. This required extra effort and took up a fair amount of spare time. Another thing I learned was that the people in class had an expectation of me, my character, and my lifestyle, which was beyond my own standard. Because I had come to care about them, I felt pressure to change in my private life. An example was when two older men from the church asked if I would consider serving as a deacon.

"What would that mean?" I asked.

They told me of the work and of the routines of deacon meetings. They also mentioned that a deacon was expected to live by the congregation's covenant, one aspect of which was abstinence from alcohol.

Alcohol had not been a big part of my life. I sometimes drank with friends in college, but Gwen did not drink. When I became a doctor and a father, an occasional glass of wine as a dinner guest in someone's home and offered by the host was the extent of my imbibing. I told the men from church that my life was so crowded with patients and daughters I did not have the time to meet the obligations of being a deacon. However, my conscience continued the conversation, and I asked myself, *What about drinking?* The one-way conversation continued: *The people you care about and whom you are teaching seem to think you are qualified to be a deacon. They probably also assume that you go along with the church covenant and don't drink.*

I had not thought of my occasional drinking wine as mattering until this little encounter. I decided that if the people who thought of me as their teacher held me to a higher standard, I could either meet it or disappoint them. So I decided to raise my standard.

I don't include this tale to argue a point about drinking alcohol but rather to bring into focus two scriptural warnings for teachers that guided me: "Let not many of you become teachers, my brethren, knowing that as such we will incur a stricter judgment" (James 3:1) and "Pay close attention to yourself and to your teaching; persevere in these things, for as you do this, you will ensure salvation both for yourself and for those who hear you" (1 Timothy 4:16).

I became used to a stricter judgment in college when I was regularly inspected in detail. I lived for four years in barracks as a cadet and learned not to leave my little room without looking in the mirror. Each part of my uniform had to be properly presented at all times, and my room was always subject to inspection.

For four years I lived by a code of conduct and a strictly enforced honor system. I was taught to practice personal accountability without complaint. If I was justly and accurately charged with an offense, I was expected to formally confess in a written agreement, then to accept the consequences with a proper attitude of submission.

In medical school, when the information came so continuously that I was forced to streamline my learning practices from college, the learning often pushed me beyond my intellectual and technical competency. Yet my character and personality always were part of my performance evaluation. During that time, I learned to practice the professional standards expected of doctors. The lines of tolerance for failures of both competency and character were contracted even more tightly in residency.

When I began my practice in Charleston, I was not the clueless, undisciplined high school graduate of fifteen years earlier. All of this preparation was before becoming a Bible teacher under a "stricter judgment." So I accepted that judgment as well; and with it, I understood that personal change was a necessary part of the work, as I tried to resolve inconsistencies of truth between the science and the scriptures I was teaching. But I did not anticipate wonderful, new insight into child-rearing and fatherhood as my professional years unfolded.

The issues of my patients often challenged me to find solutions for the crises of their parents, as well as to figure out how to raise my daughters better. Almost daily I heard the same complaints of children who wouldn't listen and children with bad attitudes. Remembering how much medical school learning came to me simply by understanding the words of the teachers, I began to ask myself, *What exactly do parents mean when they use words like* listen *and* attitude? With this question in mind, I prepared my Bible lessons.

The first time I connected the wisdom of scripture to practical child-rearing was when I was teaching through the book of Amos. There I found a quotation of God speaking as the Father of the nation of Israel to His child (that is, the people of the nation): "For I know your transgressions are many, and your sins are great" (Amos 5:12).

In preparing to teach this passage, I was struck by the two words: *transgressions* and *sins*. In English, it would be simple to say that the verse is expressing the same thought twice; that the two words are of equivalent meaning. But in the Hebrew, *sins* are misbehaviors—spoken words and actions that are morally wrong and miss the mark. *Transgressions* are the evil intentions of the human heart that misalign a proper relationship and energize misbehavior.

This insight led me to reexamine the words of parents whose children wouldn't "listen" and who had "bad attitudes." To parents, *not listening* meant not obeying, a problem of behavior. But *not listening* was not the same as a *bad attitude*, a fundamentally wrong alignment with the status of an individual in authority.

My medical training taught me the psychological concept of behavioral modification as a means of correcting misbehavior. But attitude is a theological issue of the heart, and God, not science, is the expert on aligning human hearts. Years later, I realized that my own heart would have to change before I could truly help a parent restore a child who had a bad attitude.

Becoming a Child of God

I cannot remember ever doubting that there was a God and that He loved me. When I was young, I had a sense that He watched over me and was aware of my coming and going. I also knew that I had an obligation to Him as my Creator, and I would regularly pray that He would "help me to be a good boy."

When I was about eleven years old, I asked Jesus into my life. In maturity, I knew that God was my spiritual Father through my relationship with Christ, but my prayer life was sporadic. I confessed when I was aware of a mistake, and I often gasped for help in times of need, such as passing impossible academic examinations. My policy about that part of my life was that I would be responsible when I messed up an exam and when I passed one, I thanked God.

From this background, I had a practical, business relationship with God. This changed dramatically in my first year of practice after some drama in a newborn nursery. On routine early morning hospital rounds, a nurse approached me at the nursery door and asked me to come to an Isolette where a premature baby had just died. I was not the doctor for the baby, but I was the only doctor in the nursery at the time. So I began the newborn resuscitation protocol I had learned so well in residency.

I was skeptical of success. But over the next hour, the nurse and I were able to first restore the baby's life and then stabilize it for transport to the neonatal ICU at the university hospital. Because of the circumstances and other demands on my time, I failed to register the baby's name in my mind and I had only a momentary conversation with the mother as I rolled the Isolette away to the elevator.

The following Sunday, my pastor offered a prayer for a newborn who was in critical condition at the university NICU and for the doctors and nurses who were trying to rescue the little one. I realized then that the prayer was for the baby I had worked with, and the family must be in the church. (It was a large congregation, and I was a new member.) I had not experienced many mystical moments in my private life with God before. But in that moment, somehow, I awakened to the living God working through me and in my life.

The following Sunday, I heard a sermon centered on a verse I had memorized as a four-year-old: "For God so loved the world, that He gave His only begotten Son, that whoever believes in Him shall not perish, but have eternal life" (John 3:16). The verse was not new to me, but what I heard for the first time that morning was the little article *in*; it was whoever "believed *in* Him" and not merely *about* Him.

Over the next months, I began to truly believe what I had been taught since childhood. The word *in* described where I was with Christ and where He was with me. From this experience, Jesus became a reality in my daily life. He is the divine person *in* me who exists alongside me. He wants me to know about the Father who created me. He watches over all the history of my life and gives me a father's responsibility for the two little girls He also created.

As I saw more and more clearly that my Creator was also my Father, I began to connect many new dots through my experiences with the girls at home and with my patients in the office. The God of the Bible is the Father of our Lord Jesus Christ. He is also the Father of His stubborn child, the nation of Israel. More personally, He is the Father of people like me who are His adopted children. Our Father empowers His children to understand and perform as parents under construction. God is the perfect parent, and He knows all about child-rearing.

My Father connected with me again one day soon afterward as I was driving between hospitals and turned on the car radio. A Bible teacher was quoting a question asked by Jesus: "Do ye not therefore err, because ye know not the scriptures neither the power of God?" (Mark 12:24 KJV). I agreed out loud, "Yes! Yes, that is why I err. I know not the Scriptures neither the power of God!"

I began to immerse myself in Bible study as I prepared my lessons for Sunday, noticing repeatedly that God speaks in the context of Father with those who are His own. With Jesus, the Son who always and only wants to do His Father's will, He maintains a relationship so perfect that theologians speak of it as Trinity. With the nation of Israel, He is always the patient and faithful Father of the prodigal son, watching and waiting at the same door the son had earlier closed behind him as he left home. To imperfect, adopted children like myself, He offers insight and power to change and conform to the perfection of the model of the Son of God. This person, Jesus, was in me, teaching me to conform as He did.

I then faced the dilemma that had been developing in my inner life of understanding since college. Countless teachers had taught me biology, physiology, and psychology, training my brain to process truth as a scientist. Many medical doctors had taught me how to draw rational conclusions from the observations and facts I had confirmed. Now, I was confident that I had encountered my true teacher, who had waited for me to show up in His private tutorial class.

When I was a child, a favorite Bible story was of Daniel and his friends, who were captives of the king of Babylon. The king's purpose was to select the best of the young men of Israel and groom them to eventually join his native advisers as *wise men*. This preparation included offering them the rich royal menu of foods which went beyond the diet prescribed by Jewish law (Daniel 1:3–17).

Rather than compromise, they challenged their supervisors to let them prove that the diet prescribed by the God of Israel would produce in them all the king desired and more. The supervisors reluctantly agreed. In the end, the king was impressed that the food of the God of Israel had produced in them superior health and wisdom.

As it was with the young men of Israel in the court of Nebuchadnezzar, I sensed that I also faced a decision about whose food I would accept. I decided that my Father, the Creator of children, would have answers for me as a father and counselor which I could be sure were true.

I continued to study advances in pediatrics and remain qualified as a member of the hospital medical staff. I regularly learned in continuing medical education courses, and even after more than thirty years of practice, I passed again the pediatric board exam. Meanwhile, debates swirled about the innate morality of children, the superiority of societal norms to private parental standards in child-rearing, and the suspicion that the Bible contained outdated and even dangerous advice for parents.

I decided that I no longer would accept the premise of psychology that parents cannot be certain of truth, so they must limit themselves to helping their children discover their own truth. I decided to no longer eat from the king's menus. I would choose the nourishment from my Father's table.

Becoming a Teacher at Home

By the time I finished residency, I had learned how to be a student. A student is a learner. I didn't realize then that the challenge for the rest of my life would be how to be a teacher. A teacher is one who imparts a lesson. It is not enough that the teacher prepares the lesson or presents the lesson; teaching is only accomplished when the lesson is actually implanted in the mind of the student.

Imparting a lesson requires effective communication. When the lesson is communicated verbally, a peculiarity of the way our minds work in conversation can interfere in imparting the lesson. In the moment of speaking, we tend to concentrate on the thought we are trying to express and not how we are connecting to the other person. If that connection is lost, miscommunication and misunderstanding often follow. If the connection is to be restored, the correction always begins with confession and an apology.

Conversation works on two parallels. One is the obvious plane of verbal information being exchanged; the other is the more subtle exchange of emotions and attitudes, revealed by tone and volume of voice, choice of words, facial expressions, and posture. I first recognized my own periodic failure in communication in my professional work when I became angry or developed an attitude with a parent or a nurse. The subtle habits that betrayed my bad attitude in the moment were offensive to the other person but were usually unrecognized by me in the best of circumstances. I was ready to improve.

Since I usually missed mistakes in my conversation at work at the time they happened, I made a private commitment to write a note of apology when I became aware that I was offensive. My embarrassment in acknowledging my failure became a stimulus for me to watch my end of professional conversations more closely.

Then I saw the evidence of the same problem in conversation at home with my girls. I realized my own harmful cues would have to be overcome before I could correct the whining, arguing, grumbling, and sullen performances of my children. But I needed a referee to flag the "offside" plays, and often, only my young children were present in the moment.

My solution was to tell the children that when I got mad at them, I was wrong. (I'm sure they already suspected that, but they seemed amazed that I would admit my error.) "If I speak to you in a way that is not good or act like I'm mad, I will be wrong, and I promise I will always tell you that I am sorry. If I'm so mad at you that I can't say, 'I'm sorry,' I will be wrong *twice*. Then, I will tell you I'm sorry twice. Also—and this is important—I want you to tell me if I speak to you in a bad way and don't tell you I'm sorry."

That began to work because they seemed determined to point out my mistakes. But they could not have been as determined as I was. Degrading myself to the point that I would ask for the correction of a child became a huge incentive to change.

In our modern use of the term, an apology is more than just an excuse or explanation. Most people are not satisfied unless an apology comes with an expression of true regret. When I told the kids I was sorry, I wanted them to see and hear that I was sincerely sorry. By modeling a contrite moment, I hoped that they also would experience the relief and joy of forgiveness when it was their turn to confess.

Apologizing to my children had a transforming effect on me. It caused me to confront my inadequacies as a father and realize that I had problems which, if uncorrected, would likely affect my little girls. My impatience and attitude lapses usually resulted from certain misplaced priorities that I was beginning to see were not in line with the call of my heart to raise up my children well.

In a real sense, my anger could be understood as a part of me that was still immature. I would not be successful in leading my children to maturity unless I grew up first. I had to stay ahead of them in my own maturity. They were watching me. Sincere apologies for mistakes, along with practices of correction, were the key to growing my own character. It was an example for them as well.

Having experienced the reality of change and a higher level of emotional maturity in myself, it occurred to me that apology and repentance was a principle by which all of us mature. So I committed to a policy for my children: when they were mistaken in conversations, I would hold them accountable and wait for their apologies and recommitments to improve. When one of them lost her temper or showed a bad attitude, I would close down my conversation at the moment, whether at the supper table or in the car. If an apology was not immediate, she would have to deal with her stubborn streak in isolation. The stubborn streak would invariably evaporate each time through the miracle of a contrite spirit produced in the privacy of solitude. In the meantime, as I waited, I would pray for the change.

During this season, a couple we had known in pediatric residency in Atlanta visited us. We had all become parents at about the same time. They had a young daughter, and we spoke of professional experiences, child-rearing, and our own parenthood. Then I broached what I had learned about apology leading to maturity.

I was surprised that my fellow pediatrician thought I was wrong to accuse my young child of something that would make her feel guilty to the point of needing to apologize. He said that her "sins" did not deserve such a severe reaction from me and that I could not be sure I was right and she was wrong.

I answered, "I believe God gave me my children and holds me accountable for their upbringing. I must judge them accurately, and so I believe that He gives me the insight and ability to deal with their hearts." At the end of the day, we were friends who agreed to disagree.

Having realized that I was the teacher of my children under God's authority and by His wisdom, I began to learn about teaching in the home. The lessons came rapidly, one of the first being the insight that children are naturally neither reliable students nor skilled workers; they needed to be trained to listen. This insight came one day when Gwen asked, "Who wants to learn to bake chocolate chip cookies?"

The girls ran into the kitchen. There followed a few minutes of quiet, then noise. In a moment, the girls ran by me with Gwen close behind, shaking a spatula. They had eaten the chocolate chips.

I considered the facts (as a scientist might) and then unwisely said to my wife, "You asked the girls 'Who wants to learn to bake chocolate chip cookies?' But you were actually trying to make chocolate chip cookies at the time. If you want to teach how to bake chocolate chip cookies, it doesn't matter if they eat the chocolate chips so long as they learn to bake the cookies. On the other hand, if you want to *make* chocolate chip cookies, you shouldn't ask chocolate chip eaters into your kitchen."

She just growled, and I privately considered further what I had observed. Children must be trained to be students before they can receive lessons, just as they must learn how to do jobs before they can reliably do work. Oh and sometimes, spouses aren't in the mood for a lesson either.

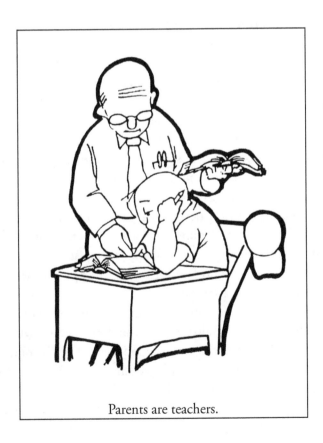

Parents are teachers.

Becoming a Servant

The demands of bugle calls throughout my freshman year at The Citadel trained me to conserve and use the moments of my day. I was expected not only to keep my uniform and room straight but also to maintain the uniforms and rooms of certain upperclassmen. This, in addition to keeping up with academics, consumed much of my time.

On cold mornings, five of my minutes were used to warm up the toilet seat for a senior heading for medical school after graduation. Early on each frosty morn, I would scoot down to the latrine just before reveille and take a seat. Like clockwork, a few minutes later, the senior I was serving would shuffle through the door and call out my name. "West! Where are you, boy?"

"Sir, I'm down here on the last seat, sir."

He would appear at the stall and tell me to get out of there. I would, as he opened his morning newspaper and occupied the warmed-up seat. I guess this was hazing. But in truth, I considered it normal in a place that I never really understood. The standard of never being late and the demands of each moment kept me focused, and I am glad for the experience. It did not occur to me until years later, however, that beyond learning about using time wisely, I had also learned how to be a servant.

A servant has to be competent in the expected work, or he is of little value. A servant also accepts his lower status with a good attitude if he wants inner peace. A good servant is distinguished by competency, humility, and cheerful submission as he lowers his status and places the other's needs ahead of his own.

Humility is a state of being in a lower status than others; humiliation is the emotional experience of stress associated with being lowered in status. (A person *is* humble but *feels* humiliation.) I eventually became proficient at shining shoes and sweeping floors. But the wall I had to overcome in being a servant was myself—I had to profoundly give up my *right* to personal time for the sake of others.

As the winter mornings melted into spring, I came to enjoy those few minutes in the latrine, sitting quietly and waiting before barracks life heated up for the day. Learning to prevail over the powerful negative emotions in the barracks would one day contribute to my being an effective physician in a medical crisis. My mornings on the can prepared me for moments in the delivery room when I would stand masked and gloved, waiting quietly for the obstetrician to arrive, while the fetal monitor warned that the unborn baby's condition was deteriorating.

A servant is no more useful than his control of his own emotions; dealing with the stress of servanthood is part of the work of a servant. In my first few years as a father, I knew that I was properly in charge as a teacher and leader. I asserted this authority not only by speaking commands but also by modeling proper behavior and conversation.

If my daughters came to understand me as the guy who bossed them around, it seemed logical that they would learn how to be bossy. With this in mind, I practiced thinking before speaking, just as I had been trained to do years earlier. When my child was in a teachable moment, I spoke a direction or taught a point of guidance. If she was not, I worked on our relationship and somehow endured or finessed the urgent requirement of the moment.

Lowering my status to the level of a servant was counterintuitive, but I wanted the girls to find their ultimate roles as servants for others. Eventually, I understood that effective teachers are competent servants with lessons to impart. I came to realize that maintaining the heart of a servant in the lives of my little girls was essential to success, just as it was essential to success as a doctor.

I practiced showing my attitude of a lower status at home, patiently reading the same bedtime stories and singing the same songs over and over as requested. During these enjoyable evenings, I could impart ideas without the urgent demands of getting a job done. I learned to accept a level of harmless nonsense without comment as I practiced reticence in conversation because a good servant stands by, watchful and quiet.

The joy of those moments and our closeness made words of correction and encouragement linger in the air. That joy also compensated for my vain hope for more interesting evenings. In accepting my status as a servant to my girls, I found peace, just as I had learned to be serene in the latrine at college.

As a doctor, I knew emergencies when I saw them. I was trained to respond to them according to certain priorities. For instance, an unconscious baby may have a heart that is no longer beating. But a heart that *is* beating does no good unless oxygen is in the lungs, so breathing is the priority before the heartbeat. Breathing cannot occur unless the airway is open, so positioning the head is the priority before the first rescue breath in a resuscitation.

A blue baby is different from a spilled glass or mud on the carpet. I may not have been in the ER, but I learned to accept that I was still on call at home. From this practice, I discovered a principle: my home life was virtually without true emergencies. My policy as a father became "There are no emergencies at home. I always have time to think before I speak." Not speaking until I had first considered the circumstance and my child's alignment with my authority resulted in a marked improvement in reliable obedience.

Parents fulfill their roles as servants to their babies as they feed, bathe, and change diapers. But this surrender of personal status to the needs of a helpless baby can eventually scream out in protest as the child grows and still demands service. This is because we so easily fall for the false notion that free time is a personal entitlement.

The unpleasant feelings of stress can lead to mistakes, such as ignoring the child's immaturity and demanding an unreasonable performance before he has been trained in the work. Because of these mistakes, we might find ourselves asking the question, "When are you going to stop acting like a child?" It is then that the unspoken answer convicts us: "I will stop acting like a child when you require me to listen and then practice with me until I have learned to listen."

Parents are servants who have lessons for those who will listen. It is out of our humility, not our threats, that we assume authority over our children. The commandment to "honor your father and your mother" is one of the most important teachings for a child to practice. The secret of teaching this commandment, though, is a paradox, expressed in a proverb: "The fear of the Lord is the instruction for wisdom, and before honor comes humility" (Proverbs 15:33).

When I was a lowly freshman, that senior cadet claimed sovereignty over my throne on cold mornings. Years later, he was an accomplished surgeon, serving alongside me on a hospital staff. I was honored in that time to be the pediatrician for his child. We laughed at the role he had played in my journey toward becoming a competent doctor who eventually advised him and his wife on child-rearing troubles. As I tried to conform my policies to biblical wisdom, I began to see that learning to be a servant who had warmed a toilet seat with the proper attitude of humility and respect warmed us both in the end.

Becoming a Coach

When I was young, I had two good friends. I could play with either of them, but the parents of one of them would not permit their son to play with the other boy because his parents were divorced. This standard was not unusual for that time. But societal norms were changing dramatically when I was beginning a career in pediatrics and learning about fatherhood.

One stark moment occurred soon after the Supreme Court's ruling on "a woman's right to choose." A young teenager was brought in for medical attention because of morning sickness; my suspicion was confirmed by a positive pregnancy test.

I privately asked my patient if she wanted to tell her mother or preferred that I introduce the discussion. She asked me to take the lead, so I brought her mother into the examining room and broke the news. The mother became agitated and emotionally distraught. In an attempt to console her, I said, "I know that this is a disappointment for you."

With bitter tears, she replied, "I just wish I had the right to an abortion fifteen years ago when I was a pregnant teenager."

In those years, much of my professional time was spent counseling broken mothers, betrayed fathers, and clueless grandparents who were trying to raise children without basic stability in their family situations. Meanwhile, in the news there was much discussion about the topic of *family values*.

Pastors and political leaders seemed to agree that family values mattered, but I don't recall an agreement on exactly what family values were or how they were best promoted. Pastors spoke of biblical standards, linking family values to political issues such as divorce rates and abortion rights. Politicians were concerned about costs and government programs. It seemed to me that most people were talking around the topic but not about it. Meanwhile, in the trenches of the culture wars, I saw parents lose confidence in their abilities and concede child-rearing to day care workers and schoolteachers. These, in turn, seemed more concerned about meeting professional standards than in training children.

Somewhere along the way, we lost an old idea: a young child should be trained at home to be a student; he should be practiced in the disciplines of a student before entering a classroom. Meanwhile, many children were being set adrift. They were left to devise their own standards, set their own courses, and cope as best as they could.

As for values, I learned a simple definition for the word: "Values are what's important." I also learned that values were not necessarily taught in a classroom, but were *caught*, like a contagion, through close contact. I also realized that the loss of family values would have to be solved in homes, not in day cares or Congress. Family values mattered to me as a father, so I enlisted as a soldier in the culture wars within my own family.

Both Gwen and I recognized that we had a number of values we could trace to our parents, such as enjoying reading and wanting to teach others. But generally, we could not recall these values being specifically taught in our homes as children. What we did recall was listening to our parents and not resisting their authority.

They must have trained us to listen when we were very young because we could not remember repeatedly resisting their authority. This is the sense of a scripture for parents: "Train up a child in the way he should go, even when he is old he will not depart from it" (Proverbs 22:6). The Hebrew word translated as *train* is usually translated as *dedicate* in other verses and connotes conceding your child to God's oversight as you make your contribution to the effort. Doing this includes both nurturing and oversight of practices in a careful order. The etymology of the Hebrew word can give an image of an animal, perhaps a horse in a corral, learning to first accept a bridle, then a rider.

The phrase "in the way he should go" in the Hebrew can translate to "according to his way." This has the rich meaning of "in the way this *particular* child should go *at this time*." A two-year-old is not a six-year-old for sure. But also, *this* two-year-old is not *that* two-year-old, and this two-year-old will not stay this way for long.

The advice of the proverb is to know your child so well and practice with him so much that *in this moment*, you know the way *he* should go. If you do this and trust God, your thoughtful direction will stay with him, and the Lord will guide him from there.

By this wisdom, I realized that biblical standards such as "children obey your parents" and "honor your father and your mother" would require more than merely telling the girls what to do and then getting upset when they failed. We actively trained our young children to listen by practicing with them and then testing what they had learned. If I could coach my own children to routinely accept my teaching authority with a good attitude and to practice what I taught, maybe some values would be *caught* in the process.

Since I was their teacher, I needed to reexamine the way I understood teachers. The vast number of teachers I had known through my years of education seemed like ranks of faceless soldiers marching toward me in their columns, touching my classroom days briefly, then passing on. I really didn't know them as individuals, and I felt sure that most didn't really know me either. Few ever took me aside and worked with me.

Teaching two little girls would be a different kind of teaching. It would be more like a piano teacher sitting beside the student on the bench or a batting coach standing at the plate with the batter. This was closer to the meaning of the Hebrew word most commonly translated as *discipline* in the Old Testament. Discipline is learning by doing, practicing doing something right. Discipline requires authority to maintain order, but the authority is asserted in a context of working alongside each other. This is discipleship teaching, the classic method used by Jesus. Discipleship teaching is instruction by practice in the context of fellowship.

Understanding that my teaching would be in a discipleship setting, I realized that my children were not yet reliable disciples. So the work of those first years was to train them to reliably listen. If they always listened, they would always be teachable. It was an ideal more than a practical possibility, but I was committed.

I was concentrating on training them not to bother each other, but how did this promote *family values*? Jesus taught His value—what was important to Him—when He said, "A new commandment I give to you, that you love one another, even as I have loved you, that you love one another" (John 13:34). The great distinctive of love is kindness, and I wasn't sure how to teach the sisters to spontaneously help each other without my prompting.

I had been intentionally dealing with their relationship for a year when Alice received a dollar as a birthday present from her grandmother. The dollar gave her an itch that could only be scratched by spending it on a yellow helium-filled aluminum balloon with a big happy smile.

As she held her new prize, a bomb exploded for two-year-old Julie. There was no way to explain to her about her big sister's birthday money and the balloon. I had blown it. I could have predicted that Julie would react badly to her big sister's advantage. But Alice, not me, saw the solution. She handed her little sister the string, and it was over. How did that happen? Who taught her that? I could only guess that she must have caught something from the coaches—her parents—who were training her in the right way to go.

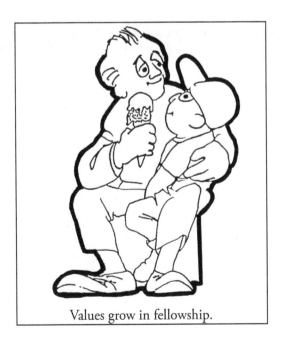

Values grow in fellowship.

PART 2

Coming to Terms with Child-rearing

WARNING: Engage brain before opening mouth.

For as the rain and snow come down from heaven, and do not return there without watering the earth and making it produce and sprout, and furnishing seed to the sower and bread to the eater, so shall My word be which goes forth from My mouth; it will not return to Me empty, without accomplishing what I desire, and without succeeding in the matter for which I sent it.

—Isaiah 55:10–11

Words of Life

I doctored and taught in some strange places. One of the strangest was the rain forest of eastern Ecuador. There I lived with aboriginal Amazonians who, forty years earlier, had been headhunters. Before the coming of Christian missionaries, the murder of an enemy and then shrinking of his head cured the curses that made them sick. Their reputation as killers was legendary. Only a handful remained when I was with them because the tribal groups had decimated each other.

Communities were organized by families, close relatives living in isolated settlements. Since I could not speak their language, I communicated through a missionary nurse who lived with them. Tribal men whom the missionaries called *health promoters* effectively assisted me with the clinical work in spite of the communication barriers.

In hours of bright, hot sunlight and predictably brief, violent downpours, I saw patients until the dramatic conclusion of each day: the shadows of the towering Andes mountains to the west brought on night almost in a moment, as the sun set beyond them. In the absence of electricity, the Milky Way provided the light at midnight.

In the communities, I was fascinated to watch a father practice the use of a blowgun with his son or a mother weave palm fronds alongside her little girl, gently handing her a few for her own little project. Other parents spoke in soft, murmuring sounds to their children as they plucked a chicken for lunch or prepared thatch for a roof. I was fascinated by the way they carried on, nurturing with words I could not understand. In conversations as old as the forest, the parents were speaking as they had been spoken to when they were young. Dominating children with parental authority seemed simply not to be part of their family culture.

As I watched these people in their remarkable lives, I realized that the parents had authority, but it was not established by threat. Rather, it was based in their humility and shared interest of staying alive. Without seeming to notice and with minimal conversation, the parents modeled survival skills and patiently worked alongside their children, practicing the routines made necessary by the unforgiving jungle. All a parent needed was a willing student; all the children I saw seemed willing. I never heard a parent speak in a tone that sounded as though it would command obedience. *Young children were thriving in the Amazon jungle without their parents barking commands and telling them what they had to do!*

In the evenings, I offered devotionals to the health promoters. They seemed to appreciate biblical thoughts about child-rearing. But I doubt that they followed ideas of coerced control derived from ancient rabbinical teachings and continued today in many modern and traditional cultures. In an unforgettable teaching moment, I commented that in my brief time with them, I had not met a *chief* or a person in leadership, and I had not observed a parent direct a child by speaking a command sternly. I then asked, through the interpreter, if anyone in the community ever told anyone else *what to do.* They looked solemnly at one another and agreed that the answer was "No."

In contrast to my friends in the Amazon, American parents tend to be far more talkative, speaking commands without awareness. Unreasonably, many also seem to assume that their toddlers—*without insight or training*—understand what they were commanded and accept that they must submit. We begin this casual use of commands with our babies, not considering that the little one doesn't automatically regard us as authority figures. He is not even aware that he has subordinate status in the relationship. This lack of consideration eventually has consequences. I learned this the hard way.

Three-year-old Alice and I had a frequent exchange at the supper table. The subject was the health advantages of vegetables. As a principle, Alice didn't like vegetables. This became apparent when I offered her some pureed carrots when she was four months old. She momentarily ruminated, then grimaced and spit them back at me with an ungarnished opinion.

As the offerings and stalemate continued, I tried placing the loathsome produce in the middle of the spoon, then dipping the front tip into some pureed pears. That, too, was dismissed. I persisted and so did she.

Then she was three. "Eat your vegetables," I would say.

"I don't like vegetables."

"They're good for you."

"They taste bad."

"They make you strong."

"They stink."

As was my professional habit, I analyzed the case to understand a diagnosis. Eventually, I moved from the thought of vegetables and their benefits to the realization that she was learning at the supper table a lesson I did not intend to teach. Regardless of my honorable intention to teach principles of a healthy diet, my little girl was learning how to successfully argue me to a standstill. I was actually teaching her that she could challenge my authority and prevail. More astounding, I offered practices in resisting my authority by commanding, "Eat your vegetables!"

Our repetitive, obnoxious conversation was actually a bad script that we had both memorized like actors in a dramatic rehearsal. Why you should eat vegetables seemed to be the rational concern. But on an emotional level, the unspoken message was, "Let's just push each other's buttons." So the unpleasant, nightly conversation continued.

Children learn the art of conversation in the home with familiar people. By age two or three, many children have learned how to say "No!" because they hear it said to them so often. They have learned bad scripts because their parents practice with them. The sorry result of not correcting repeated bad conversations comes soon enough in the teenage years. Young children may actually be comforted by our attention as we talk to them excessively, even though our tone is unpleasant. Teenagers, on the other hand, are aggravated and offended when we argue and nag. They may become reclusive and sullen or explosively angry because of our bad habits in conversation.

Everyone benefits from healthy, effective conversation, but excessive talking is often associated with *not listening*. In the home, it is often not noticed by the individuals primarily involved. But parents can help each other recognize and overcome the bad habits of verbal noise scripts and ineffective commands. Success can help the child and also strengthen the marriage. The wisdom of scripture is "Let no unwholesome word proceed from your mouth; only such a word as is good for edification according to the need of the moment, so that it will give grace to those who hear" (Ephesians 4:29).

Authority

Authority is the capacity to command obedience. But obedience doesn't necessarily follow a command. When a command succeeds and obedience occurs without applying coercion, that is proof of *effective* authority.

Authority is based on a difference in social status in a given situation, such as a policeman at an intersection or a drill sergeant facing a squad of recruits. In adult life, such authority is usually understood and assumed. This is because of previous experiences which have caused the person submitting to recognize and accept his subordinate position in the relationship. But when parents command the obedience of an infant who has neither the insight nor capacity to obey, they are unintentionally sowing seeds that one day will lead to the common complaint: "My child doesn't listen to me."

In the first months of life, a difference in status is irrelevant to a baby. Babies are helpless and clueless, while parents are usually quick to meet every need without requiring the baby's cooperation. In this time, an effective parent is merely an eager servant; it is a time to simply serve and cherish the child.

Words of authority spoken in those first months are not only ineffective—they are not rational. Babies can't possibly obey spoken commands before they have insight into authority and language and before they have developed some self-control. They can, however, be immunized to parental authority in these months of immaturity.

The uninterrupted enjoyment of fellowship *with only nurturing words* is natural. It is also gold in the bank when used wisely. It creates a memory of a kind voice, a future incentive for the child in conflict to return and restore the relationship as the voice waits in silence. Meanwhile, using commands before a child has insight and acceptance actually produces an unnecessary and ultimately destructive tension in the relationship if the untrained child does not simply submit.

A normally developing eighteen-month-old toddler may speak a dozen words and may understand even more. But he usually hears far more conversation than is useful and processes most of what he hears emotionally rather than rationally. When the words speak commands, the commands easily blend in with all the other nonsense. Not knowing the meaning of the words, he may hear commands such as "Don't touch that!" and "Leave that alone!" disguised with nurturing terms of encouragement. If he is unable to distinguish the ones that require obedience and left to guess at the meanings of terms he does not recognize as commands, he lives by trial and error.

So a parent tells his toddler to "do something." When he does not, the parent says it again, perhaps louder; the toddler still doesn't. Finally, the parent becomes agitated, tells him to do it, and then actually does it for the child, fussing the whole time.

"Come here! I said come here!"

Then forcefully grabbing the child, he brings him here, as he says, "When I say come here, you come here!"

From this, the toddler learns that if he waits when the parent says, "Come here!" he says it again (the child likes that), gets upset (usually entertaining), and eventually does for the child whatever is being commanded. Meanwhile, the child never obeyed.

A preschooler with a limited vocabulary cannot yet reason well. So if he responds to a command with the question "Why?" he is not seeking information; he simply likes to hear us talk. Our reasoned reply may make sense to us, but it must not be sensible to the child because he again asks, "Why?" Meanwhile, we have lost track of our original intention. We were expecting obedience but are now settling for an unhelpful conversation. As for our child, he will learn that asking "Why?" is how to delay obedience.

A command should invariably result in obedience, not further conversation. If there is conversation, it should occur before the command or after the obedience. Commands followed by arguments necessarily result in delayed obedience (or no obedience), along with the poison of bad scripts and bad feelings.

An embarrassing script conversation between me and my pre-schooler, Julie, concerned a stray cat at our back door. It never left because Julie wanted to keep it, and in my naiveté, I dreamed that she would learn lessons of responsibility and commitment. Julie was fine with my high purposes. I suspect that she was also encouraged that I had failed to notice that I was speaking with my imaginary child who, in my dreams, followed my directions.

In the next months, our repetitive skirmishes over feeding the cat always seemed to concern the lack of a rational reason other than my insistence that "I am in charge." The cat would be fed by Julie eventually, usually with a muttered opinion. But the next skirmish kept coming because cats keep returning hungry, and I was doing nothing to end the script.

From Julie's point of view, my direction to feed the cat interrupted her life and her plans. Probably even more important, she resented that I was dominating her free will. Children who react negatively to commands can be deeply offended when they are told what to do. In fairness though, none of us really like being told what to do.

The wise parent remembers his young child's language limitation. Someday, the older child will have more mature insight into language. But even then, memories of emotions elicited by the parent's voice echo from years earlier. When this happens, he may react emotionally rather than rationally, as he did when he was a toddler, hearing but not understanding. The parent's words may be soothing or harsh, wise or foolish, but they all carry an emotional impact far beyond their original, plain language meanings.

The assumed inequality of status that establishes the authority of parents over their children is certainly justifiable. But parental authority is no more than an elusive assumption until the children are trained to obey commands reliably. Our enjoyable conversations build relationships, but fewer words tend to enhance parental authority. When we have problems with listening, often the reason is we are talking too much.

A missionary in Africa who heard me teach when he was a young bachelor told me years later that when he became a father, he had followed the sense of the teaching. He said he had successfully trained his infant to follow commands. Since I would usually advise against using commands with very young children, I asked how he had found success.

"We did not speak commands," he replied. "We used sign language."

No spoken words! I congratulated him on discerning such a great innovation.

Very young children can be trained to respond to authority properly and consistently. Such training may take time, but the dividends keep coming as the years pass. Much more time is required when children are inconsistent and authority is not effective. This is the message of one of the most well-known proverbs: "He who withholds his rod hates his son, but he who loves him disciplines him diligently" (Proverbs 13:24).

The Hebrew word translated *rod* is *shebet*. This word usually speaks of the scepter of the king in other passages. The parents' status is far beyond the young child; their relationship is like that of royalty with a subject. The young child needs to be disciplined—trained— to respond with obedience to commands. *"I say it, you do it"* is the critical first teaching of the parent who loves him.

Listening

When I was young, I loved the Bible story of the child Samuel. My favorite part of the story was when he was asleep in the temple, and the Lord called to him in the night. Samuel answered, "Speak, for Your servant is listening" (1 Samuel 3:10). I identified with him as my teacher taught that we should all be like little Samuel and *listen*.

The Hebrew verb translated as *listen* actually translates both *to hear* and *to follow a direction*, that is, *listening is hearing and doing*. A more complete definition of Samuel's listening would be *hearing, understanding, and obeying. This is what parents are thinking when they tell their children to listen: hear me, understand me, and obey me.*

As a father, I reread the story (1 Samuel chapters 1–3) and considered how it was that Samuel came to listen. Samuel was the long-awaited first child of Hannah. She was so eager to be a mother that she promised God she would give her child up to serve Him if He would bless her with one. So the Lord gave her Samuel, and *"the woman remained and nursed her son until she weaned him"* (1 Samuel 1:22).

Samuel was probably around three or four years old when his parents turned their little boy over to the high priest of Israel. He lived out the rest of his childhood in the temple with Eli, his foster parent. So how was it that when Samuel was a middle schooler, he so simply and wonderfully *listened*, first to Eli, then to God?

I believe that Hannah must have first trained him to listen to *her*. Then she taught him to accept the authority of future teachers like Eli as well. By practicing listening under his mother's supervision, Samuel had learned consistent *listening*—that is, *obedience*—at home before he went to live in the temple. Such simple home instruction is the basis of hope in sending off your child under the authority of a first-grade teacher.

Obedience is the prompt, efficient, cheerful, first-time compliance with a direction. Most parents have agreed with this definition as an ideal, although many have been skeptical that the definition is realistic. "Prompt, efficient, cheerful, first time." It's all there. The definition includes

1. when obedience begins: now;
2. how obedience is done: well;
3. what attitude is maintained: good; and
4. regard for the authority figure: once is sufficient, without question, or argument.

Samuel was a remarkable boy. Because he was trained to listen by his mother, he "was growing in stature and in favor both with the Lord and men" (1 Samuel 2:26). Children do not intuitively know to listen; they are *trained* to listen. Learning to listen is the beginning of practicing obedience. Presuming that a child will perform a task before he has first learned to listen is the beginning of disappointment and interruptions in relationships. The sooner a child learns to reliably listen, the quicker he will learn wisdom and the right way to go.

"NO!" means 'Stop! And stay stopped!'"

Practicing Listening

I t is possible to train some children to consistently listen before they are a year old. But most parents do not consider this possibility; rather, they just begin giving their children commands. Usually, commands given to young children are sugarcoated so as not to alarm the child, at least initially. Spoken in the rhythm of normal, quiet conversation with a baby and minimizing the verbal volume and clarity associated with authority, commands are often not distinguishable from the rest of the words that are largely nurturing but not yet understood.

Infants are not rational in their thinking and have very little insight into adult thoughts and conversation. Their vocabularies are extremely limited, and if they understand some words, the understanding is concrete and primitive. Even if an infant has insight into the intention of a command—that it is supposed to result in his obedience—he is not likely to understand an explanation of why he must obey. Yet parents explain *why* to their young children.

"Open your mouth and eat your carrots," says (commands) a mother, holding up a spoon to her nine-month-old at the table. "They're good for you and will make you grow big and strong" (*why*).

The baby doesn't know words like *open* and *eat* and doesn't know that he has just received two commands to obey (*open* and *eat*). If he opens and eats, it will not be the result of obedience. It will happen because he sees the food, is okay with the taste and texture, and is hungry.

Even if a nine-month-old recognizes a command spoken distinctly with authority, he still may not obey because his will is contrary to the command. Then he may experience the unpleasant feelings produced by chemicals in his little body when his will is denied.

These chemicals of anger drive an emotional response that can dominate his consideration of obedience. The drama of his emotional response can then cause a parent to back away from insisting on the definition of obedience. *Not listening* results.

Giving a command to a child is risky because no one, not even an infant, likes being told what to do, and commands often produce stress in relationships. We all have a notion of our free will and are aware when a command challenges our desire to do as we please. (Some of us are still stubborn, even as adults.) Meanwhile, *though authority can command obedience, it can also invite conflict.* The bonds of relationships are threatened when authority introduces the probability that the will of one human may be dominated by another's will.

Ideally, an infant at around nine months can be trained to listen fairly easily if the child has not been confused by ineffective commands. In a moment of no tension or time pressure, a parent can place the infant within reach of a forbidden object that is attractive yet safe. When the child shows an intention to reach for it, a single word of command—"No!"—is spoken directly and firmly. "No!" alone transmits the command to stop, stay stopped, and give up your will.

If this is a practice in listening, the forbidden object will now become the focus of practice until the baby loses all interest in reaching for it. The practices are always done when the child is rested and without needs, and the parent is not distracted by the rest of life. (The phone is off.) When the training is successful, the child can be left in the presence of the object without considering it further. Then the next forbidden object can be introduced and listening practiced again. In the end, a one-year-old can have a policy of "You say it, I do it" as rules are thoughtfully added. That's good!

Listening is
- Hearing
- Understanding
- Obeying

Obeying is complying with a direction
- promptly
- efficiently
- cheerfully
- first time

Not Listening

I heard it every day in the office: "My child doesn't listen to me." I had previously heard this complaint in residency, but no one told me how a pediatrician should answer the problem. I was too busy learning about medical issues to deal with this common child-rearing issue. Now I was supposed to know the answers. So I determined to pay closer attention to the stories and to the children interacting with their parents as they came into the office for medical reasons.

It seemed that some children listened, as though listening were a part of their nature. Other children, though, seemed stuck in an unstable tension with their parents' authority. Parents with more than one child believed that *listening* and *not listening* were natural temperament traits expressed in the individuality of their children. I agreed. From infancy, Alice simply went along with my direction while Julie seemed predisposed to challenge me.

In my preparations as a Bible teacher, I began to better understand the foundational scripture for parents, "Train up a child in the way he should go, even when he is old he will not depart from it" (Proverbs 22:6). "The way he should go" no doubt is the way of biblical wisdom. But the words translate a Hebrew phrase that actually reads "according to his way." When I considered this, I realized that all children should go the way of wisdom, but kids who naturally listen go a way that is different from those who don't.

The child who listens may go on and on with instruction about the right way to go in life. The one who doesn't listen, though, cannot reliably receive further wisdom until he is trained to consistently listen. *Not listening* is a symptom of an underlying problem, like *not sleeping* and *not taking a bottle*. A symptom is not a diagnosis but rather evidence of a problem. I needed more information to understand the problem.

First, I confirmed that the parents agreed with the definition: *listening* meant *obedience* and *not listening* meant *disobedience.* Then I considered the differential diagnosis of *not listening* in a list that would help uncover the various reasons for not listening and lead to solutions for particular cases.

A child may not listen because of an undiagnosed hearing problem, or he may be too young to understand language or to control himself. Since listening requires insight into authority and competency to respond, not listening may be due to the child's lack of discernment. Finally, the child may simply be expressing a contrary will. So the reasons for not listening are

- he can't listen—he can't hear or lacks some critical physical, intellectual, or emotional capacity, or is otherwise without self-control;
- he doesn't understand—he is without language development or experience with authority;
- he has been trained not to listen—he practices habitual disobedience because of unintentional bad practices; and
- he will not listen—he has a bad attitude and has set his will against the authority figure.

With this differential diagnosis of *not listening* in mind, I began to observe individual children who failed to listen. It didn't take long to see the answers for parents directly in front of me in the examining rooms. With this new understanding, I decided that Julie would not be raised the same as the way I raised Alice. I loved them the same, but they were not the same people, and I would respect that fact.

Reasons for Not Listening: Can't Listen

Most babies with hearing deficits and born in American hospitals are identified in the newborn nursery. Babies with communication disorders are usually not diagnosed until later in infancy when normal baby sounds and words are absent or delayed. Other medical conditions associated with an inability to *listen* include brain disorders and injuries and conditions such as central auditory processing disorder. Attention deficit disorder interferes in following sequential commands such as "Please take your books upstairs, and bring down the laundry!"

Of the many babies with normal hearing who are nonverbal after eighteen months yet seem to understand language, most will be talking before the next year passes. This variant of *normal* language delay is especially common when an older brother or sister is in the younger child's life and speaking on the child's behalf. Some young toddlers, though, will eventually prove to have important communication problems such as autism spectrum. Not hearing and not being able to process and produce speech are on the list of why a child can't listen.

Much more commonly, though, not being able to listen is a problem in social development. Many mothers begin a quiet conversation with their babies before they are born. The tender words continue through the newborn period, and soon, the babies associate particular voices with nurturing. Such one-way conversations often include questions like "Are you ready for a bath?" as well as descriptions of activities, such as, "Let's see if you need a diaper change." These sentences may end with question marks or periods, but a baby is unaware of these points of grammar, and besides, the words make no sense. The baby doesn't yet know the words *ready* or *bath* and has no concept of a changed diaper. He is unaware that sentences are spoken as statements and questions. All of us are guilty of *not listening* to mere background noise.

But then words in sentences like these are mixed in with sentences that, in other circumstances, would be punctuated with exclamation marks: "No-no honey, don't push away your blanket!" or "Stop kicking while I put on your booties, baby!" An English grammar teacher might require exclamation marks after these sentences because they are commands. But the words are actually received as nurturing words, murmured and cooed like all the others.

The irrelevance of giving commands to infants is obvious. But parents often tell their little babies what to do and what not to do repeatedly and without awareness. They speak commands with gentle reassurance, and it is obvious they do not expect obedience. In fact, they would be shocked if the baby obeyed. They are *just talking to their babies*.

Meanwhile, a baby hears these meaningless, one-way conversations and learns to be nurtured by words of commands. Eventually he learns how to cause the words (whatever their meaning) to be spoken by doing again whatever he was doing that stimulated the parent to speak. After a few months of this kind of communication, a mother might comment that the baby is misbehaving *only for attention*.

She is right, of course. And yet she dismisses this insight and continues the talk that supplies the attention. A child who is too young to listen and learns to associate commands with nurturing may one day not listen, even though he could.

Reasons for Not Listening: Doesn't Understand

A command is the statement of a rule that must be obeyed. In the military, an example of a command is "About, face!" When this command is given to a soldier at attention, he turns around and faces the opposite way. Within hours of beginning my freshman year at The Citadel, I learned that commands were given in two parts, separated by a momentary pause.

I was trained that if I was standing at attention and heard a command that began with the word *about*, there was only one word following. That word was always *face*. The word *about* told me that I would momentarily be turning myself around. The pause that always followed was to allow me a moment to process the meaning of the command before I was required to obey. When I heard *about*, my brain would prepare me to move my feet and shift my weight so that I could whirl around to face the other way.

In this two-part way of speaking a command, there is a principle: obedience is enhanced if the command can be rationally considered first. The practical application for children who are being trained to obey is to speak a *preparatory* command before a *command of execution*. For instance, "In a few minutes, I will call you to supper. Sometimes you don't come when I call. It is important that when I call, you come right away. Do you understand?" Such a preparation may seem tedious, but if prompt obedience results when, a few minutes later, you say, "Please come to supper, now," it was worth it.

In my first week as a freshman, ranking cadets were training and correcting us. But soon, the full company of more than one hundred cadets had formed for a *practice parade*. Because I had never marched in the full company before, I didn't know that commands given to the company were supplemented privately by any nearby upperclassman as we marched.

One of the details to be attended in a marching company was the alignment of rifles on the shoulders. Rifles are supposed to be held at an angle, maintained by the position of the elbow and wrist. When rifles are carried on the right shoulder, all of those in ranks and files are supposed to hold their elbows at ninety degrees, tucked against their sides. They hold their wrists locked and straight. This tends to keep all the rifles aligned as the formation passes.

I didn't know this at the first practice parade. I had been told a lot of information and called a lot of names, mostly with reference to my state of ignorance, but I was never told about rifle alignment at parade. At some point, the cadet behind me hissed, "West, butt in!"

I knew I had just heard a command, but I had no idea what it meant. (*Butt in?*)

He said it again, along with some colorful, descriptive images of me and my mental fog. "Butt in!" he growled.

I had to do *something*. So I threw my hips forward as I marched, hoping that if my posterior moved in, it would correct whatever was so offensive. This seemed to only worsen the situation. Now he was raising his voice, repeating the command, and describing me in words sublime, even poetic. By spinal contortions, I threw my hips further forward. I intended to obey but didn't understand the command, and meanwhile, my rifle alignment became even worse.

This did not end well, but eventually, I learned that the "butt" of his concerns was the butt of my rifle. His will was that I draw the rifle butt in closer to align my rifle with the others. My intention was to obey, but I did not understand the command.

It is certain that younger children have variable and incomplete insight into the meaning of words. Misunderstanding the words and intention of a command is a reason for not listening. Teaching and practicing effective communication—I understand you, and you understand me—is a critical part of learning to listen.

Reasons for Not Listening: Trained Not to Listen

A command is an expressed direction which must be obeyed. "Please come to supper!" and "Go take your bath now!" are examples of commands. Commands expressed to children as questions ("Will you please come to supper?") or as information ("It's time to take a bath.") or worse, as whims ("I wish you would stop running in the house."), are often not recognized as commands. Confusing other ideas in conversation with commands and not speaking commands with a distinguishing authority bring on conflict and set up the practice of not listening.

Consider three-year-old Bradley, whose mother says that she hopes he will not run off as he did the last time they went shopping together. So when they arrive at the store, he runs off and hides under a clothes rack. I had seen Bradley regularly on checkups since he was a baby and watched as he was trained not to listen.

At four months of age, Bradley accidentally pushed against his mother's hand as she tried to release the strap on the infant carrier. "No-no, honey," cooed the mother, who freed the baby from the restraint and lifted him into her lap. Nothing from the baby. He was too young to have insight into the words and couldn't obey if he did.

Then two months later, he rolled over on the examining table. His mother reached out her hand to stop the roll, saying, "No-no, baby! Stay on the table!" She then patted him gently and sat him up.

"Let's sit up, now. That's a good boy," she murmured. Nothing from the baby. But mother's soft, reassuring voice probably reminded him of something, and it was a good feeling.

When Bradley was nine months, he crawled away from us in the examining room and reached for the wall socket. She was talking to me until this moment; now he had her attention. "No, Bradley! No-no. Bad boy!" she said with alarm as she rushed to him, picked him up, and set him firmly in her lap.

He was obviously happy in that moment, so she put him down on the floor again as we continued our conversation. We all know where he crawled off to again. She corrected him again and picked him up again to hold him in her lap. Then she smiled and told me, "He's just doing it for attention."

"That's true," I said. "Except for 'just.'"

On an eighteen-month checkup, he made a break for the door. The mother spoke loudly, "No, Bradley! I told you to be good. Don't try to leave!" She moved quickly, picked him up, and held him. He struggled against her grip. "No-no! Be good!" she commanded.

Then she cooed, "Do you want some ice cream after we're through? If you're a good boy, we'll get some ice cream."

Ice cream seemed like a good idea, but where was it? Probably beyond the door, which was still open. Guess where he went when she put him down again.

By the time he was three, Bradley was an experienced explorer and committed anarchist. As it once was for Mom, shopping had become one of his favorite activities. He knew of all the best hiding places in a store and was always eager to shop. Meanwhile, his mother wondered why she felt a sense of dread every time she pulled into the mall parking lot with little Brad.

Discipline means learning by endeavor, that is, by practice. Correctly, child discipline is training in doing it right. Whatever a child practices will be performed better. If he practices doing it right, he will become better at doing it right; if he practices doing it wrong, he will become better at doing it wrong. Commands that are not clarified and not obeyed offer practices in doing it wrong. *Not listening* then can prove that the child has practiced—but not correctly.

Reasons for Not Listening: A Bad Attitude

One of the most common questions during a well-child checkup was, "How do you deal with a kid with a bad attitude?" As the conversation continued, I would usually learn that the child was responding to commands with anything from an eye roll and sullen silence to a feral growl and roiling rage, with or without eventual compliance.

Usually, I also learned that if obedience occurred, the parent might complain of the bad attitude ("You can't talk to me like that!") yet accept the task being done as resolution. This was a mistake. The *obedience* was incomplete and, in the end, it was only deceptive proof of a change of attitude. The lingering bad attitude would explain the failure of the next command.

Some people seem to be inclined by their temperament to simply accept authority; apparently, it is in my own nature to accept authority. Growing up, this helped me to receive instruction in school, to generally follow directions, and to stay out of trouble. Teachers and other adults in my life probably thought that my inclination to accept authority was evidence of a *good attitude* toward them and their status. I don't remember my parents commenting on my attitude much when I was young—except once, after I had received my last spanking.

When I was about seven years old, my older brother and I committed some felony that in our mother's judgment was spank worthy. After the sentence was carried out, she sent us upstairs. In that moment, as we climbed the stairs, she somehow didn't seem as big and tough as she used to be, and the spanking didn't seem as awful as it should have been. My brother apparently shared this opinion, and we were snickering together when Mom sternly said, "Stop!"

We did. Then she looked squarely into our souls and said coldly, "I'll never spank you boys again. Go to your room!"

We did. And she didn't. In my life, she was in charge, and I don't remember another moment like that.

I first became aware that others cared about my attitude when I was a freshman at The Citadel. As I was standing in a rigid, exaggerated *brace*, cadets with authority would approach to within an inch of my eyes, which were locked on a distant nothingness. With a suspicious squint, they would peer deep inside (as my mother had done), seeking my opinion.

In psychology, attitude is the alignment (or misalignment) in a relationship that results from an opinion of either approval or disapproval. A bad attitude may be concealed and privately held. But emotions percolating within can expose the secret opinion to others through conversation, facial expressions, and body language.

In the Bible, an attitude is a *mindset*, a point of view of the heart. The Greek word *phroneo* translates *attitude* or *view* (compare English translations of Philippians 3:15). The origin of the word is related to the diaphragm, the great muscle that contracts with each breath and is close to the heart.

Our attitudes are inseparable from who we are at the deepest level, and God knows that is not always good. When waterlogged Noah offered a sacrifice after the flood, the Lord observed that "the intent of man's heart is evil from his youth" (Genesis 8:21). Jeremiah sounded like a parent when he asked, "The heart is more deceitful than all else and is desperately sick; who can understand it?" (Jeremiah 17:9).

The Creator of children observes that "foolishness is bound up in the heart of a child" (Proverbs 22:15), and surely a child's bad attitude is the proof of foolishness. But if attitudes are the result of harboring an opinion, it seems unlikely that the youngest children are guilty of deep thoughts when they stand against parental authority. Toddlers don't seem to have deep thoughts.

The younger the child, the more likely that a grumpy or defiant behavior is based on a temporary, unpleasant emotion or physical discomfort like hunger or needing a nap. Even in older children, disobedience and anger in response to commands may be disrespectful but not necessarily due to a fundamentally bad attitude. The disturbing emotions of stress and the unexpected alarm of a psychological trigger in a moment can result in behaviors that look like a bad attitude but are actually explained otherwise.

For instance, a school-aged child who is the victim of a bully or who has lost a best friend may develop a bad mood that spills into the parent's life as irritability, contention, and defiance. This may not be manifested as a bad attitude until Mom asks, "Have you finished all your homework yet?" or Dad says, "You need a haircut." For some, a bad attitude may arise from no more than a minor disappointment or change of plans, which actually is more likely to be an expression of fear of the looming *unknown* about to happen.

Bad attitudes often result from assuming a false status in a relationship. For instance, if a child assumes unjustified authority, he may then perceive disrespect and take offense. This is common with children who watch their parents, older siblings, and teachers model their superior status every day. The child can easily imagine that he is in charge like everyone else and develop a bad attitude when his commands are challenged.

Resistance to authority is often the big issue of attitude for parents. Attitudes and relationships are commonly tested when a person of higher authority speaks a command. The obedience of children to the directions of their parents is specifically commanded in scripture, and *listening* can certainly be critical evidence that the child is properly aligned with authority. But proper manners are also possible with a bad attitude. (Think of a prompt and efficient but surly waiter in a restaurant.)

It is parents, not children, who must awaken an awareness and then the behavioral habits of a good attitude, at least in the beginning. Children need to be trained in *proper* conversation and manners so that they learn to sense in themselves the way their attitudes are directed.

When a *meltdown* that looks like a bad attitude actually is a need for a nap, remaining calm and solving the compelling problem of the child is the simple fix. But when a bad attitude is deliberate and even premeditated, it is a spiritual issue with a spiritual solution.

Attitudes are a matter of the heart, and the transforming work of our Father focuses on the heart because "from it flow the springs of life" (Proverbs 4:23). If our attitudes as His children matter to Him, the attitudes of our own children ought to matter to us.

A bad attitude is a loss of alignment.

Apology

The origin of the word *apology* is the Greek word *apologia*. But this word is almost never translated *apology* in English Bibles because in the Greek, it is a verbal justification or explanation. In our culture, we would consider an apology which only explains *why* as incomplete and unsatisfactory. We want to know whether or not there is contriteness and regret, along with a commitment to reform.

I learned the details of a full apology as a cadet because The Citadel was a place of rules that were broken. Even the most diligent and well-intentioned cadets found that it was almost impossible not to violate a rule occasionally. Often, breaking a rule required submitting an official *apology* to the commandant. This typed statement was known as an ERW (Explanation Required, Written).

According to the ERW form, the cadet would first restate the charge, such as "absent class" or "unauthorized visitor in room" and then state simply that the offense reported was either *correct* or *incorrect*. This critical part of the apology was basically an opportunity to *confess* and agree with the charge. (The word *confess* actually means *agree*.)

Following the statement of agreement or disagreement was the written explanation, the *apology* of the ancient Greeks. This prose could sometimes soar to sublime heights, or it could simply be "You got me. I got nothing." The third element of the ERW would be especially scrutinized. Here, the cadet selected one of three statements: (1) "The offense was intentional," (2) "The offense was unintentional," and (3) "There was no offense." His choice, subject to the unforgiving search of the Honor Code, would reveal his attitude.

Years later, I developed a more complete understanding of confession and apology from Julie when she turned thirteen. In this time before cell phones, her grandmother gave her a telephone as a birthday present. As we connected this landline phone to the jack in her bedroom, I said, "Honey, there are some rules. I may need the phone at any time for my medical work. You must let me have the priority when necessary. Also, you can make no phone calls after nine in the evening, and you can't use your phone to call boys privately. Okay?"

She agreed.

That evening, her best friend joined her for an overnight as part of the birthday celebration. Late in the evening, my wife told me quietly, "Julie and her friend are in her bedroom, talking to a boy on the phone."

"I'll take care of it," I replied and went on to bed. I knew that Julie would be energized to resist me at midnight on a sleepover and that she would not be in good condition for a discussion about the phone until she could recover from the all-nighter. A confrontation in the moment would be noisy and likely end in a stalemate.

So out of respect, two days later I said, "Julie, I want to speak to you about your phone. You and your friend were on the phone at eleven o'clock two nights ago with a boy. I am taking the phone from your room for two weeks so that you know I mean business with my rules."

"That's not fair," she said. "It wasn't me who made the call. It was my friend."

"That may be, but you were responsible for the phone, so I'm taking it for two weeks."

She protested strongly again, now in her lawyer manner. "That's not fair! You didn't say that my friend couldn't make a call."

I knew her well and had encountered her attorney before. "You knew it was wrong. Why else would you make the call from your closet?" (She didn't know I had that bit of evidence.)

"Humph!" she said. "It's still not fair."

At this point, it was apparent that her phone etiquette was no longer the issue—it was her attitude of disrespect. So I countered, "Because you broke the rules, I'm taking the phone away for two weeks. Because you don't agree that you're wrong, I'm taking the phone away until you agree. Then the two weeks will start."

Regardless of whether a disrespectful offense arises from a simple mistake in manners, a bad mood, a bad attitude, or even from evil intent, the solution always begins with an apology. This is common sense; it is also basic New Testament teaching. When the offender seeks a pardon in a sincere, contrite spirit, authentic forgiveness *(letting it go)* can resolve the issue.

Months later, on Father's Day, Julie sincerely confessed and apologized. "Thanks, dear," I said. "That's the best Father's Day present you could give me. Now the two weeks can start."

After a week of a good attitude and no complaint, I told her, "You've done such a good job this week, you can have the phone back now. Please remember the rules."

To clarify, I don't remember there being tension in our relationship during that half-a-year trial. She seemed to accept my authority easily and showed no evidence of a bad attitude. Her apology wasn't about breaking the rules so much as it was about slipping around my authority and then hoping I would connive with her. Her attitude, not her misbehavior, was my concern. A contrite agreement and apology was the solution, and I refused to connive.

The word *connive* is from the Latin word that means *to wink.* Children generally are the wrongdoers; it is the parents who *wink.* I wanted her to understand that I would not participate in her quibbling and would not accept her bad attitude, an unspoken opinion that her status was no less than mine.

I spent time in prayer during those days of waiting. I knew that my capacities as a heart doctor were limited, but I could call a consultant who really knew the score. Between Julie and me, the issue was about finally and truly accepting my authority. I wouldn't force her to accept it. In my life experiences, I had seen coercion fail too many times with children. I did not understand the mystery of God's activity in her heart. But I trusted it and did what I could, waiting and hoping.

Julie lost the phone for two weeks because she broke the rules; she lost it for six months because of her attitude. When her attitude was realigned and she could appreciate my mercy, she confessed and got the phone back a week early. It is important to mention that mercy is for the contrite; a child with a bad attitude interprets what is intended as mercy to be weakness and will see an opportunity to exploit. The words of the prophet are haunting: "The heart…is desperately sick…who can understand it?"

The heart condition of a bad attitude can be chronic. If it is not truly resolved, its symptoms will continue to surprise you in the most inconvenient moments. It keeps playing into the quality of your home life like a clown with unlimited cream pies who rents a room down the hall. You know he's there, but maybe not this morning. Maybe I could walk down the hall now, and he won't be there.

Maybe so. Then again, maybe not.

You know it's coming—don't be surprised.

Respect

One memorable moment for me as a doctor in the Amazon rain forest was a skit, presented in the twilight of a community hut. Two men were demonstrating the conversation that would occur between warriors who unexpectedly encountered each other on a trail in the *old days* of murder and headhunting. The script had developed over the timeless past, and through the generations, children learned it from their elders. All who remained alive knew the script.

The two "actors" approached each other from opposite ends of the oblong hut, leaving to our imaginations the dense green vegetation that separated them and blocked their view.

After a few steps, they both suddenly stopped, as though sensing the other's presence. Now fully alert, they each set an imaginary arrow to a bow. The frozen silence lingered.

Then one softly murmured something that sounded like a few grunts for the interpreter, who said, "I am here."

Pause. Silence. Again, "I am here." Nothing.

Then, "I am here. You are there."

So he had located the stranger—maybe an enemy—in the foliage.

Now the other man spoke through the interpreter. "I am here." Nothing.

The first man repeated, "I am here. You are there."

Then the other said also, "I am here. You are there."

At this point, the two had recognized each other. They knew where each other was located and were satisfied that they could move forward on the trail and meet each other without violence.

Learning this script helped the next generation keep their heads when they met a stranger in the jungle. It was the beginning of understanding the other person and his intentions and then acting according to what was learned.

The jungle social ritual demonstrates the principle of the Hebrew word translated as *honor* in the fifth commandment: "Honor your father and your mother, that your days may be prolonged in the land which the Lord your God gives you" (Exodus 20:12). In this verse, the Hebrew word for *honor* translates to *evaluate carefully and respond appropriately.*

In contemporary usage, the English word *respect* has mostly replaced the word *honor*, but the meaning persists in both words. Respect involves first insight then conforming behavior to the understanding with a proper attitude. As a practical example, respect is the protocol called *manners* by which a subordinate acknowledges the superior status of the other.

Parents routinely consider that respect is simply obedience. (If you respect me, you will obey me, and so since you obey me, I assume that you respect me.) But this assumption does not take into account the insight and discernment that is critical to true respect.

We usually give commands to young children either to protect them ("Don't touch that. It could hurt you!") or to accomplish tasks ("Please close the door!"). Even if the child obeys slowly, incompletely, or eventually, we tend to accept this as satisfactory, often without registering whether or not he had a respectful attitude in the process.

The assumption that obedience means respect is deceptive. A young child's obedience is usually due to his recognition of the difference in status between himself and his parent. The parent is bigger, stronger, smarter, and more competent to force his will. The child who obeys regards this difference in status but may have obeyed because of fear rather than the thoughtful consideration of respect.

True respect includes both insight and behavior. Insight may be years in coming, but when we teach our preschoolers socializing behaviors considered to be *good manners*, we are teaching an unspoken principle: "You are too young to understand me and respect me. But you are not too young to regard my authority and to begin *acting* as if you respect me. Someday I hope you will know me and respect me.

But for now, if you just listen, you will know how to act when you do respect me."

Obedience may be evidence of respect, but respect is not the same thing as obedience. If respect requires insight into the other person, how much insight into his parents can an eighteen-month-old have? Can he know of the hours of planning, the sleepless nights of worry, and the financial costs his parents have already invested in him? Can he know of the joy, tears, and prayers?

In truth, respect for parents is simply not a possibility for young children. If a child develops respect for his parent, it will only be after the passage of time—years, even many years. It will also be a function of insight obtained through conversations and education, leading to knowledge controlled largely by the parent.

Some parents think it best not to let their growing children into the archives of their private pasts—not to share family stories, why you never see your grandmother, what happened to my sister in that old photograph of us. Some parents think that their children should not know what happened to them in the war or why they must take medicine every day. Some shield them even into later life from how they dealt with the depression from a lost job, the anger over a failed previous marriage, or concerns they have about paying for college.

Hardships and tragedies occur in all families. Sometimes the feelings arising from the events of life are almost unbearable. Young children without the experience and personal character resources to understand and cope must be protected from the emotional impact of these crises as much as possible. Also, it is true that a foundation stone for maintaining authority is fostering an element of mystery in the way the person of status is viewed by subordinates. This is part of the explanation for a *teacher's lounge* at school and an *officer's club* on a military base. Similarly, holding on to certain undisclosed parts of life help maintain a parent's authority. But family intimacy thrives in an environment of mutual trust, and prying open at least some of the boxes in the attic can be worth the risk.

Stressful times are a part of adult life. A wise parent can, and should, find appropriate teaching opportunities for children as they are able to handle them. Older children can be helpful players to some extent in family troubles, and a crisis can be an opportunity for promoting maturity if the parents can prevail over their own fears and grief for the sake of the children. During crises, the older child can discover the true character and faith of the parent who is willing to risk being vulnerable.

Permitting the gradual and thoughtful exposure of a child to the heavier issues of family can happen over years of home life and conversations. He can experience a gradual awakening to the complexities and dilemmas of adulthood without being overwhelmed by the emotions. He can learn to avoid the pitfalls of *bottling up* bad feelings, prejudices, and grudges.

Respect is based on an accurate knowledge of the other person and conforming behavior and conversation to that understanding. By inviting my child to intimately join me in life as he grows older, he can respect me not only because of my strengths but also regardless of my weaknesses. He can also learn of his value to me and how much I care for him.

Respect for Children

In the decade before I retired from pediatrics, I became interested in learning what is known as *addiction counseling*. Thirty years of practice had awakened me to the impact of adult addictions on the children who lived in the home.

My parents did not drink, but as I grew up on naval bases, I was aware of alcohol. When I was ten, I had a friend whose parents thought it was funny to give wine to their pet parakeet and then watch it try to fly while under the influence. Occasionally, I visited homes of friends whose parents were flying no better than that parakeet.

I was sometimes around sailors with drinks in their hands. On one occasion, I was with other kids at a *ship's party*, near a long line of celebrants approaching a beer keg at a swimming pool. My parents were in the line and almost to the keg when my father called to me. He bent down to my ear and said softly, "Go get in trouble!"

I did. (It wasn't difficult.) So just before they reached the keg, both of my parents excused themselves from the line to take care of business with me at the crime scene. Then they returned to stand at the end of the long line. I was aware that they never reached the keg.

My parents rarely spoke to me directly about moral decisions. The moral instruction I received in Sunday school and Boy Scouts was the standard they held and probably assumed I would follow. Alcohol was not part of my mother's family. I was aware that my dad's father imbibed on the rare occasions that we went out for supper with him. I don't remember my parents ever speaking of the *evils* of alcohol or telling me that I shouldn't drink. I did think that beer smelled bad.

I left home for college as a teetotaler. During the second semester, I learned to escape from the alarms of the plebe system for a few hours on a weekend by drinking beer. Without instruction, I figured out my limits by trial and error. But when I returned home for the summer, my mother awakened me to the consequences of adult decision-making. A twenty-something friend across the street invited me over to shoot some hoops in his driveway and afterward offered me a beer. A little later, I plopped down beside my mother on the couch at home. Apparently after taking a whiff, she looked at me and said, "You know I disapprove of alcohol." I never was around my mother again with alcohol on my breath.

The truth of this moment is more complicated. I believe my mother and father must have thought that I would discern their standards without explanation or discussion. But I was truly clueless as a child. Maybe because I usually did well in school and mostly stayed out of trouble, my parents assumed I wasn't naïve. But I was.

After years of counseling with parents, I see now that my parents' assumption about me was a typical misstep for all of us. They were relating to me as their imaginary child, the kid I ought to have been, who knew what I should have known and acted as I should have acted. I think they mistook my capacity to behave myself and receive teaching as evidence that I actually had discernment. I may have been a *good boy* most of the time, but I actually dwelled in the fog of what my wife calls Edward-land. (She, by the way, knows me well and would have nothing to do with an imaginary husband.)

I often recognized imaginary children in the office by the question posed by their parents: "Why would he do that again?" When a parent continued asking *why* about repeated mistakes, an imaginary child was usually the culprit. Sometimes the mistaken identity was profound, and I could see the hurt on the child's face as the parent spoke. I actually felt sadness when I realized I was talking to the parent of a child he or she did not really know.

Young children fail to meet their parents' expectations for many reasons. When the failures occur, parents can say things that are hurtful because the child of their imagination wouldn't do what this kid just did. Even young children can perceive that their parents do not accurately know them because of their surprise and disappointment at repeated failures. The misery of this error can be the origin of a long descent into poor self-esteem, apathy, and dysfunctional coping. But even worse, a child may conclude that his own parent does not respect him. In the end, a sullen resistance and a sour bitterness may be all the child can produce.

The parent who is distracted with memories of *how it was when I was your age* will not only make mistakes as he forgets the reality of the present moment, he may also set himself up as a target. Children recognize when we do not deal with their reality, so when they misbehave, they begin to count on our irrelevant and ineffective responses. They eventually develop a distorted view of who *we* are. Instead of mature, wise teachers who direct them in the right way to go, they come to see us as nuisances who complain and threaten. If we continue to disrespect them for who they really are, our teenagers will begin relating to imaginary parents.

The solution for the imaginary child starts with a counterintuitive conversational move into the real child's life. Not an interrogation but a true back-and-forth about *you and me*. Since the parent will not enhance his reputation as an authority figure by continuing an ineffective harangue, perhaps the conversation should begin with a confession and apology. In a golden moment of connection, it may sound something like this: "I guess you've noticed I have been on your case lately. I am wrong to harass you, and I am sorry for when I get upset and speak to you with angry words. I love you, and I want us to be close. I hope you will forgive me."

If the need is to obtain the child's respect, there is no single move more effective than a contrite apology with honesty and humility. Many parents avoid apologizing to their children in the false notion that an apology is evidence of weakness. The value of modeling a contrite, sincere apology in the opening conversation easily outweighs any risk of embarrassment and the momentary lowering of status. This is the wisdom of the proverb "Before honor comes humility" (Proverbs 15:33).

Not unlikely, the child in this circumstance owes the parent an apology as well. The parent initiating the reconciliation is offering himself as a model for the repentance which will restore the child. Having apologized, the parent can continue the conversation with confident authority. "I have been wrong. I am sorry and ask your forgiveness. But I am still your parent and you owe me an apology as well. I hope you will apologize too."

It is at this point that a wise parent might reintroduce his status by saying something like this: "I can wait for your apology, and you can wait in your room until you're ready to rejoin the family."

Your imaginary child comes with a pie.

God's Respect for His Children

It is not unusual to have the impression that God was rather grumpy in the Old Testament and somehow mellowed in the New Testament. In Genesis, the Creator seemed to have an easy conversation with Adam, but things changed when Adam failed to *listen*. From that point, the relationship between God and humanity deteriorated. By the time of Moses and the captivity of the nation of Israel in Egypt, God seemed remote and severe.

It was Moses who first revealed that God was the Father of the nation of Israel. But the people of Israel openly challenged God's authority and violated His commandment almost as soon as He spoke to them through Moses. So ironically, when the time came to tell the people that God was the Father of their nation, it was also the time to tell them that they had failed as His children. The Jewish rabbis teach this revelation as the "Song of Moses," a poem from his deathbed. In it, God is praised as the Father who delivered them from slavery but whose children were not worthy to be called His children:

> Give ear, O heavens, and let me speak; and let the earth hear the words of my mouth. Let my teaching drop as the rain, my speech distill as the dew, as the droplets on the fresh grass and as the showers on the herb. For I proclaim the name of the Lord, ascribe greatness to our God! The Rock! His work is perfect, for all His ways are just; a God of faithfulness and without injustice, righteous and upright is He. They have acted corruptly toward Him, they are not His children because of their defect; but are a crooked

and perverse generation. Do you thus repay the
Lord, O foolish and unwise people? Is not He
your Father who has bought you? He has made
you and established you. (Deuteronomy 32:1–6)

God has always respected His children as individuals. The
divine Father knows each of us to a depth far beyond human capacity
and responds to us righteously. None of His children are imaginary
to Him. The psalmist sings of the Father, "You scrutinize my path
and my lying down, and are intimately acquainted with all my ways"
(Psalm 139:3). He knows that "the intent of man's heart is evil from
his youth" (Genesis 8:21) and that "foolishness is bound up in the
heart of a child" (Proverbs 22:15).

Yet the Father relates to each of us properly, even when we are
not straight with Him:

The Lord has recompensed me according to
my righteousness, according to the cleanness
of my hands in His eyes. With the kind, You
show Yourself kind; with the blameless, You
show Yourself blameless; with the pure You show
Yourself pure, and with the crooked, You show
Yourself astute. (Psalm 18:24–26)

In history, God selected certain individuals to receive knowledge of Himself. Abraham was called a "friend of God" (Isaiah 41:8;
James 2:23) and "the Lord used to speak to Moses face-to-face, just as
a man speaks to his friend" (Exodus 33:11). David was distinguished
among the writers of the Old Testament by his relationship with
God. He came to know God so well during his trials in the desert
that he marveled, "Your gentleness makes me great" (Psalm 18:35).
These great figures of the Old Testament were privileged to know
God because God took the initiative and revealed Himself to them.

Then Jesus came to the children of God to "explain Him" (John
1:18). It was Jesus who promoted the value of children (Matthew
19:14) and first taught that the God of Israel wants to be known to

each of His children as Father. When the children of Israel requested that Jesus teach them how to speak with their God, He replied, "When you pray, say: 'Father…'" (Luke 11:2).

My parents had a solid marriage. My brothers and I knew that they were on the same team and that they considered us individually. My mother was small, fun, and easy in conversation. In spite of her size, she was also effective with authority. In my father's absence, my mother was clearly in charge. My father and his wonderful attributes were a common topic for my mother and me as we talked over the dishes in the sink.

My mother was the main source of the deep regard I held for my father's authority and the respect I hold for him today. Physically, he was a big man and looked impressive in his naval officer's uniform. Even when I was just a little guy, I don't remember his voice being raised in our home, and he never hurt me. But I was always aware that he was in charge, and I was not.

As I matured, I learned much more about my father, but it wasn't by his input. My respect for him (my insight into him) grew by my own curiosity about who he was and what he did. I don't think he intended that he remain obscure to me; he was so humble that he may not have thought that my knowing him was important. Now I know that I missed out on a special conversation that would today be a treasured memory.

In my own family, by what I have learned of my heavenly Father, I decided that I would have a different approach with my own children. I want them to know who I am. Not because I have an overactive ego but because, as the fifth commandment comments, so that their days "might be prolonged" (Exodus 20:12). Also because it is the model that God gives His children as their Father.

Rabbis today teach that God is the Father of Israel but not that He is a personal Father to individuals in the nation. Without Jesus, such a relationship is a theological impossibility. For Christians, Jesus makes the connection, like the way my own mother connected me to my dad. As for Jesus, "He came unto His own, and those who were His own did not receive Him. But as many as received Him, to them He gave the right to become children of God" (John 1:11–12).

God has gone to great pains for us to know Him, even as He has preserved His boundaries. In a similar way, we should want our children to know us. "Therefore, be imitators of God, as beloved children" (Ephesians 5:1).

Children need it—parents have it.

Learning Disrespect

On a teaching trip to Africa, I met a diminutive woman with too many grandchildren living in her one-room home on a dirt floor. Her sons were truck drivers and mostly gone; the mothers of the children lived nearby but worked long hours and were not around most of the day. The children's ages were three to twelve years old, and they seemed to operate together as a pack, led by the older kids.

In western Uganda at the time, public schooling was usually made available only to one child in a family. I was supporting a ministry that was offering more educational opportunity for children in the dramatic Rwenzori Mountains on the Congo border. My job was to teach child-rearing to pastors in conferences and to parents in local churches.

Through an interpreter, the grandmother asked me how to make her children return to her home after school. Then she told me her story. "Each morning, I tell them they must come home after school, but they do not listen. They go to the homes of other children. They finally come home for supper, but they are not there to help me carry the water, so supper must wait. Then they are unhappy because they are hungry. I tell them I need help with the water for supper, and they promise to come home each day, but they never do. They will not listen to me."

"Do they love you?" I asked.

"Oh, yes," she smiled. "We are all very close. Sometimes, we all sleep together. They want to be with me, and we are always talking about many things." Then she asked, "But why won't they come home?"

The answer was difficult for her to hear. She was a grandparent who was actually in the role of a parent. She was fussing away her authority. Her children were learning to disrespect her as she improperly *enabled* them, even as she ineffectively nagged them.

Parents must tenderly provide for their children as well as keep them safe and direct them in the right way to go. Nurturing, intimate conversation can come with a price in the loss of authority. On the other hand, words that are effective in obtaining obedience may come with the price of severity and the loss of fellowship.

The nurturing parent who feels stress arising from this dilemma might relieve the uncomfortable feelings by lowering rules and standards while nagging. The authoritarian parent might find release through angry words and harsh punishment. Either of these solutions can cause the children to misunderstand who their parents are.

In the case of the African grandmother, she had a rule: "Come home after school." When the children failed to do so, she would complain, but this would not change their disobedience. The children enjoyed her conversation as they folded her nagging words in with nurturing words.

It's only grandmother whining again, they might think. *She complains but doesn't require obedience. Supper may be late, but we always get something to eat eventually.* They disobeyed her today because she tolerated their disobedience yesterday. Tomorrow, their disobedience will continue because of the reputation of toleration she has established. Her reputation for indulgence today fueled their disrespect tomorrow.

It was sad, but she had actually taught them to disrespect her. They knew that she cared about them and that her commands could be ignored. They did not know her as the dignified woman she really was, and they had no insight into her status or authority. This lack of insight developed because she had a servant's heart, and servants may not exercise authority very well.

The children responded to her as they knew her; they were disrespectful because she had tolerated their disobedience. It was exaggerated as the older children modeled patterns of disrespect to their younger siblings. Their conversation was likely similar to schoolchildren waiting for the bus and discussing teachers and their reputations at the beginning of the new term.

For the grandmother who had very limited resources, a complicated social circumstance, and a hill to climb before making supper, restoring her reputation was a priority. Her children were at different ages and so would have to be considered individually in a counseling plan. Babies, who begin clueless about their parents, become young children who draw conclusions about their parents and others in the family. Ultimately, reputation will be the final determinant of respect or disrespect.

Children learn fairly quickly about standards and expectations in different circumstances. From a school-age child's viewpoint, the older people in the family may seem confusing, unpleasant, and sometimes even scary for reasons unknown. But at least these characters are familiar and the chemicals of bonding compel the child to want to be near them. So children adapt to their assumed status according to their temperaments and pressure from older people in the home. Without effective direction, they cope by doing whatever works in a moment.

The grandmother wanted the best for the children, but she had lost her reputation and so could not effectively direct them. I suspected that after years of practicing the habits of a gentle nurturer, she probably did not have the energy or the commitment to change and become an effective authority figure. So the project became to develop her strongest suit—her popularity.

After explaining that repeatedly fussing was only making things worse because the children enjoy the attention and hearing her talk, I asked, "Do the children like bananas?"

"Oh, yes," she said. "Bananas are a treat for them."

"Can you afford to buy bananas for each child on school days?"

She said she could, so I offered a plan. Buy enough bananas today for everyone, and tonight at supper, tell them that tomorrow, you will read stories to the ones who come home from school on time, and everyone who is there will have bananas to eat. I asked, "How many of them will come home?"

"I think three of them."

"Then read to the three and join them in eating all of the bananas. When the others come home, they will hear about what happened and especially about the bananas. Of course, the bananas will all be gone because they were for the ones who came home.

"So tell them you will buy bananas again tomorrow and those who come home on time will eat them. How many will come home the next day?"

"Three more," she said with a smile.

She may not have been an effective authority figure, but she could still have her way with at least some of the children. The stress for her would be in keeping a commitment not to nag and to hold the standard of "Bananas are for the ones who come home—and there is no discussion!"

Effective authority figures maintain their reputations through boundaries that are consistently attended. Maintaining these boundaries requires vigilance, patience, discernment, and self-control. Virtues like these are tested when everything at home screams, "Gotta get the laundry done, gotta make the doctor's appointment, gotta finish the lawn, gotta…" Our children learn to disrespect us because we lose sight of what we look like and sound like in front of them. When we lower the boundaries that protect our dignity, particularly by talking too much, disrespect crosses the line.

Teaching Respect

Teaching your children respect is a lifelong project. It begins with being thoughtful about making rules and consistent about enforcement. When they are teachable, the curriculum of respect is what we know as *proper manners*. In the course of teaching, we continually evaluate attitudes, resolving issues fully and revealing more and more of ourselves in conversation.

By these practices, your children will not only move to higher levels of maturity but also grow in their respect for you. This may seem idealistic, but producing children who truly respect you is worth the time and effort. My two girls taught me these lessons as teenyboppers.

I was sitting at the kitchen table one evening when the phone rang, and I answered. It was for Alice, one of her eighth-grade buddies. I brought her to the phone. She said she didn't mind if I remained in the kitchen while she took the call. From what I heard of the hour-long, one-way conversation that followed, I thought that an hour had been lost in silly talk about nothing.

When she finally said, "Goodbye," I mentioned that she and I used to talk that way in long conversations about not much. "Why don't we talk that way anymore?" I asked.

Alice simply said, "I know that my friend will share with me just like I share with her."

I decided that night that I would change my conversation with my daughter. Between emergency room drama and family crises, my life was always interesting. I didn't need Alice's advice or consolation, but when I began telling her of close calls, amusing moments, and tense dilemmas, we began a lively conversation that went on and on. Soon, as we spoke of dealing with adult stresses and responsibilities, she began telling me of her own concerns and solutions. I could tell that she was seeing me in a new light and that we were talking more like friends.

A similar circumstance happened with Julie when she began her first semester of college. She seemed excited and confident when we left her at the campus dormitory, but within a week, she was phoning home nightly with the tears and distress of homesickness. This surprised her mother and me because we had always thought of Julie as being fiercely independent with a drive to find her own way.

In these nightly, long-distance conversations, Julie spoke of loneliness, academic pressure, bad cafeteria food, and a lack of transportation, among other things. Her mother asked questions and was tenderly sympathetic in her responses. Meanwhile, I thought that what would be most helpful from me was *active listening* with an occasional, bland reassurance.

Then one evening, she aimed a complaint at me. "Mom talks, but you never say anything to me on the phone." That stung.

I said, "You are exactly thirty years behind me when I went off to The Citadel. Your troubles remind me of my troubles as a plebe. Several of my roommates dropped out of school within our first few weeks. Then I was hospitalized with hepatitis and had to drop a course to stay up academically. It was quite a start! I'll tell you what. I will write you a letter twice a week and tell you how your experiences remind me of my college days. I'll write my first letter after we hang up tonight."

So I did. As Julie's troubles came in by telephone, my written replies went out in the mail. By midterm, her calls were less frequent and much less desperate. By winter break, she was an engaged, optimistic college coed who was saving her dad's letters for future reference, and I was a father she came to know in a new way.

True respect is based on intimate insight. These somewhat stressful moments with my daughters awakened me to a more active role in cultivating the respect of my girls. Meanwhile, I was learning more about my own childhood experiences with my parents. They did not share information from their private lives when I was a teen. By then, I had come to appreciate their loyalty and their giving without expecting repayment. But I didn't thank them as I should have, and their reticence unintentionally contributed to my unexpressed gratitude.

My stupidity still embarrasses me. I knew my father's parents were divorced, and my mother's family suffered during the Great Depression, but these things were never discussed. I knew they had faith and that my mother prayed for me, but I remember almost no talk of their private moments with God.

They would have said that I respected them because I listened to them, practiced my manners, and behaved myself. But I don't think I was very conscious of honoring my parents until after I became a father and experienced the work and stress of child-rearing.

When it was my turn, I made a conscious decision to tell my older children who I was, what I had experienced, and how I dealt with issues that one day they would have to face. I told them lots of family stories, and as they matured, they came to know many of the family secrets, maintaining a proper reticence because I taught them the importance of discretion.

I was deliberately conservative in using authority in order to maintain a cordial conversation. They knew that I truly believed the wisdom of the Scriptures I taught and that I prayed for them. Because authority and attitudinal issues between us were usually quickly reconciled, our conversations fostered the familiarity of good friends.

In most circumstances, authority undermines familiarity. But parental authority founded in friendship is a proper long-term goal. As my children grew, I practiced a certain reserve in my bearing when they were present because being their father was a primary concern. Yet our conversations were increasingly familiar and intimate, concerning a wide range of important and very personal thoughts and experiences.

Both of my girls were well on the path of personal Christian maturity by the time they left home. Years later, their conversations with my wife and me include points of theological understanding and times of mutual prayer. They cope well with the bumps of life, and we laugh a lot. I know that they respect me and that they would do anything I asked. They know I have unbounding confidence in them and their decision-making. They also know that I have no inclination to tell them what to do as an authority figure. "I have no greater joy than this, to hear of my children walking in the truth" (3 John 1:4).

PART 3

Making Disciples in the Home

"Whatcha' doin' up there, Mom?"

Hear, my son, and accept my sayings and the years of your life will be many. I have directed you in the way of wisdom; I have led you in upright paths.

—*Proverbs 4:10–11*

The Hope of Joy

When I had two preschoolers living in my home, I was also teaching other parents how to train children to listen, often in a seminar format. In one of those early seminars, I mentioned the joy of being a father. A parent attending the seminar, who was also a classroom teacher, heard something hopeful and made some arrangements. Soon I expanded this topic into the joy of being a teacher of children and presented the idea to the state public school teachers' association.

After forty years, I have learned more about this joy. I now realize that though moments of joy in fatherhood have been real, in those days, I was mostly speaking of my *hope* for joy. For many active parents and teachers, a steady state of joy has to wait because there is so much hard work to be done in the present. Many years would pass before I could truly confirm that for me, fatherhood is one of the greatest, permanent joys of my life.

From Scripture, I understand joy to be a lifting of the spirit from a heart that has been stirred. Joy is a fruit of the Holy Spirit within. It may be associated with feelings of happiness and contentment, but joy also involves the mind. It is an emotion that must be examined and thoughtfully appreciated. When it is permanent, it is based in a permanent reality.

Young children may stimulate moments of joy, but they don't intend to do this. In the first few years, they are entirely focused on their own needs and amusements. If you received a card on Mother's Day from your two-year-old, it wasn't the kid's idea; also, you probably paid for it. Your toddler has no real insight into relationships, particularly in that most critical one with you.

To your young child, you seem to just assume that he will follow the direction you determine. You also seem to assume that he aligns his purposes with yours, understands your authority, and agrees with it. You may also assume that he follows the meaning of your conversations and has the skills and self-control to carry out your will. That's a lot of assuming!

Your young child is always learning but not necessarily learning the lessons you intend. For instance, he may learn that your authority doesn't always provoke obedience and that even as you object, you still tolerate him and his bad attitude toward you and your authority. He learns that he can fast-talk you into seeing things his way and avoid, or at least delay, obedience.

He also learns that stress in his life is relieved (temporarily) by his own dysfunctional methods of coping such as delayed obedience, argument, temper tantrums, and other emotional drama. His solutions may be irrational to you ("Why are you acting this way?") yet they are natural to him and apparently okay by you because you take no action to permanently extinguish the behaviors as your bumpy relationship continues.

Without your instruction and correction, he will remain in this state of disorganization. In the absence of some curriculum designed to bring him to maturity, he will accumulate a grab bag of facts, skills, words, and experiences and try again tomorrow to make sense of things. Maybe he will even grasp a little of what is called *common sense*. Meanwhile, to him, you seem like Mary's distracted sister when Jesus visited and observed her: "Martha, Martha, you are worried and bothered about so many things..." (Luke 10:41).

Your child begins life in innocence. He is also utterly unable to add to relationships and to accomplish the tasks of daily life. If this condition is not radically changed by the end of his childhood, his inadequate coping will bring ongoing distress and pain into his adult life. He has much to learn. But if he doesn't learn submission to teaching authority, along with the disciplines of a student, he will fail with his future teachers. Meanwhile, his relationships with teachers may be repeatedly spoiled by a bad attitude toward receiving instruction, and his inclination to learn may be poisoned permanently, even beyond remedy.

There is joy in child-rearing, but it is often a momentary gasp in the midst of hard work. For many, the joy is first experienced in the delivery room when bonding can be surprisingly quick. The bond becomes tenacious for many of us, compelling tender words and ways of cherishing. Babies, meanwhile, respond in charming ways that urge more bonding.

The emotional strength of the bond is intoxicating. Habits that promote bonding are established within hours or days after birth for most parents and babies. Many babies seem to develop a fascination for their primary caregivers within a few months, and by six to nine months, they demand the continual, physical presence of these valuable providers. In these first golden months, the possibility of conflict seems unreal.

Then the commands begin: "Do-this-don't-do-that!"

The toddler must wonder, *When did I become a recruit in boot camp? What happened to the warm fuzzies?* In a relationship of tenderness, ordering a baby around, as a drill sergeant might, is a harsh splash of cold water.

A command is a rule that must be obeyed. It is not a request; it is not a whim or a dream. Supplying both nurturing and authority well requires thinking, evaluation, planning, and change. Effective parents learn to be conscious of each moment with their little one because the feeling of being joined in a natural bond of nurturing is wonderful, and the stress of facing down a contrary child is alarming.

Authority in a family is correctly founded in the strength of relationship. Authority is the expression of an empowerment. The power of authority in most circumstances is some manner of a perceived threat. (Think of the *power* a boss has to affect your paycheck or a policeman has to control your vehicle speed.)

The power that properly energizes a parent's authority is fundamentally different, and it marshals its strength early before the lessons begin. *It is the power of the bond between you and your baby that sets the stage for your authority in the next years together.*

You are a soft, inviting rose on a thorny stem. The hope of joy may be waiting for you. But the hope for permanent joy will more likely be real if you make adjustments and learn vigilance, patience, and self-control. You must also be willing to change and be grimly committed to teach until the lessons are learned. Remember, for the first years, you are *making* a disciple; if you are successful, one day he will actually *be* a disciple.

Hope is an expectation of a favorable outcome based in reality. When your hope is in the truth of scripture and in the faithfulness and power of God, your hope for joy is based in reality.

Friendship is for the future.

Teaching in the Home

Your child will have many teachers in his life, but there will not be another like you. You are the first one who gets to hold him, nurture him, and take the first shot at telling him how and why. Beyond introducing to him the skills of socializing and daily tasks, you have the first, best chance to influence his eventual values and the direction of his moral life.

The demands of days at home repeatedly compete for your attention. Your little one's capacity to receive teaching varies according to whether or not the diaper needs to be changed or he needs a nap. Meanwhile, a remarkable conversation is developing, which is one-sided because one of the parties doesn't speak the language. In fact, for a while he says nothing much beyond "goo," whatever that may mean, as he marvels about the intentions of your voice. Fortunately, your little one is wired to seek understanding, so you are the first link between him and the mysteries of the world around.

The critical curriculum of child-rearing is about the *right way to go*. In the Bible, such moral knowledge is called *wisdom*. But wisdom is not just knowledge of the right way—it is also actually going that way. For the innocent toddler, the first lessons of wisdom are necessarily about health and safety—what's good for you and what's not. You know what is healthy and unhealthy, what is safe and dangerous. Most importantly, you have a keen interest in his finding the right path in life. Without your instruction, knowledge of health and safety may be gained only by risking disaster.

Ancient rabbis taught that children are born with an inclination toward wrong and that as they approach adulthood, effective parental teaching changes this inclination toward wisdom, the right way to go. This teaching is the theme of the first chapters of the book of

Proverbs: "Hear, my son, your father's instruction and do not forsake your mother's teaching" (Proverbs 1:8). This principle, that parents are teachers who presume teaching authority and who direct their children in the right way, is part of our American culture, even in homes without Bibles.

The problem is that without the authority of revelation from the Creator of children, teaching authority in homes usually occurs as it was (or was not), modeled in the childhood homes of the parents. Many Christian parents base their child-rearing style and decisions on the way they were raised. Alternatively, in the case of unhappy memories, they deliberately reject the way they were raised but then are without an alternative plan. Neither of these choices for understanding child-rearing are particularly Bible based.

Your baby begins so dependent, and tending to his needs is such a constant requirement that it is easy to overlook your role as his moral teacher, not merely his provider and critic. He begins with no insight into your authority or language and has only a limited capacity for self-control, so if he follows your moral direction, it is because you have taught him about your authority and language and then practiced with him until he consistently listens.

With routine checkups in the office, I often mentioned the importance of taking the time to train children at home how to listen. (Training is discipline, that is, *practicing doing it right*.) One mother who particularly seemed to accept this was a nurse I worked with in the hospital. Our child-rearing discussions began on her prenatal visit. Later, with a newborn in her arms, she was convinced she would not introduce authority and commands until the baby was old enough to understand and obey.

Eventually, she told me on a checkup that she and her husband had recently first said "No!" to their baby. The baby had learned to crawl and reach well since the last checkup, and training in their home had been effective. They were gratified that the little one simply restrained herself (without their physical intervention) in that moment. She said they were anticipating going to her parents' home and wanted the baby to do well in this unfamiliar place full of temptations, including a decorated Christmas tree.

I asked if I could observe a training moment, and after they returned from their Christmas visit, I was in their home with my friend and his camera. The parents had decided that they would train the baby not to touch the video remote control that evening. They had never before forbidden her to touch it, so in the meantime, she had learned (on her own) to operate the TV with it.

The eleven-month-old was obviously attracted to the remote and would quickly select it from among other objects for play. As the training began on camera, the father sat beside the child, held the remote toward her, caught her eye, and firmly said, "No!"

The baby's face showed she immediately realized his intention, and she cried briefly. (She *really* wanted that remote control!) He then placed the remote among her familiar toys on the floor. She looked at it and quickly turned toward his welcoming arms, leaving it on the floor. He comforted her, she regained her composure, and then she resumed quiet play on the floor, apparently oblivious of the remote control.

I asked what would happen after I left. They told me they would continue to supervise practices of exposures to the remote on the floor until they were sure that the baby had set a policy of leaving it alone. It was difficult to watch the distress in the baby and to endure the moment of confrontation, but the video clearly revealed that they were enjoying their baby as they trained.

They knew that their relationship was strengthened even as they challenged her will in the lessons. They were also enriching their own place in the child's life. One day, if the child were ever to be estranged, the value of the solid bond they were forming would be the critical determinant for her return. Meanwhile, they were training the child in the first rule for a disciple: "I say it; you do it."

Just living in the same house with young children is complicated. At times, it can seem like living in a barn with irresponsible critters. Parents have reason to hope that the situation will improve. If it does, it will be because they changed and invested some hours into the project. Coming under authority, learning to effectively communicate, and developing self-control are all lessons waiting to be taught; and parents are the first and best teachers. This insight explains the mystery of why discipleship teaching—training in the context of fellowship—is so effective at home and why scripturally, the home is where wisdom is first taught.

Coaching is a picture of child-rearing.

Changing in the Home (Not Diapers)

As a parent, you are a teacher. A teacher is one who imparts a lesson. It is not uncommon for a teacher to assert some authority in a minor way so that learning can stay on track, but the authority of a teacher is limited. Teachers have the authority to determine the material to be taught and the *how and when* of the teaching. By their authority, they organize a curriculum and direct their students in a plan of study, as well as keep the minds of their students receptive to understanding.

Teaching authority is neither harsh nor coercive. Humility is the power that supports this teaching authority because a teacher is simply someone who offers a lesson to another. It is this humility that inspires respect and persuades the student to submit.

A student is a learner, one who is receptive to knowledge and practices the self-control necessary to process the knowledge. By this definition, not all of the individuals in a classroom are students. When the one offered the lesson is not a disciplined student or resists the teacher's authority, the frustrated teacher may lose his humility and compromise the teaching.

Young children do not begin as reliable students. They may always be learning but not necessarily be teachable for the lesson being offered in a moment. When the teaching of a parent actually results in learning, it is often because he has somehow prevailed over the background noise of the TV blaring, the phone ringing, the dog barking, and the older brother breaking something upstairs. The point of parental teaching is to raise the child to a higher level of maturity. This point is often lost when it is necessary to dominate and regain control in a distracting circumstance.

If a young child were to be *consistently* teachable, it is at least partially because certain measures were in place. Perhaps the most important is the training that results in the child being a consistent student, always responsive to the teacher's authority and ready to learn.

The paradox of teaching your child to become reliably teachable is obvious: if he needs to be taught to be teachable, logically he must be unteachable, at least in the beginning. This dilemma is solved by taking advantage of the fact that even a child with the reputation of being most likely to be unteachable will occasionally simply accept teaching.

If you know him and watch carefully, you can often discern a moment of his being teachable. The moment may fade quickly, so you must act decisively. This is the time to give him a practice in obedience. So you speak a simple command, regardless of whether or not there is a task that must be done: "Please hand that to me!" And he does! The task was done, but that's not the point. The point is because you said the command in the golden moment of teachableness, he *obeyed*.

If you spend too much time trying to answer the question of why he became teachable, you will miss these golden moments. You will know the moments if you watch for them, and when you see them, get *your* job done. In the times when he is not teachable, put your commands away and work on conversation and enjoying life with him. These moments of nurturing deposit memories of goodwill and are like putting money in the bank.

It is important to remember the principle that whatever he practices, he will do better. You only want practices in obedience and *none* in disobedience. You are not giving commands to accomplish tasks by his response; you are practicing obedience with him. So you must learn to time your commands to his moment.

The single most common counterproductive characteristic of parents who are having trouble with their children who *don't listen* is talking too much. Whether it is by habit or compulsion, repetitive and ineffective commands are usually the beginning of *not listening*.

Your habit of unloading commands randomly into his life may require you to change ahead of his change. For instance, your control of your own conversation is essential. When your child is not listening, you are not teaching because, in that moment, he is unteachable. If you then resort to reason or argument, he is still not teachable. If you escalate to yelling or worse, he is *still* not teachable, and you are becoming a teacher who is losing his reputation. You are only giving him practices in not listening and likely helping him develop a bad attitude.

You may have much to teach your child, but your lessons will only be imparted when he is a receptive student with self-control who cheerfully submits to your teaching authority. Training a child to be consistently teachable seems time consuming, but consider how much more time would be available if your child were to consistently listen and simply do as you instruct. It is even possible that you will one day find that you have a teacher's aide to help.

I was on the highway with ten-year-old Alice and her best friend riding in the back seat. By their occasional giggles and the few whispered words I picked up, I knew that they were speaking of something they thought I wouldn't approve. My authority from the front seat at seventy miles per hour was compromised, and an attempted correction would likely not be effective. It was not a teachable moment, so I said nothing.

That evening after supper, I told Alice that I would like to talk with her in the living room and that she should bring her Bible. Alice had been remarkably teachable from the earliest I can remember. At this age of ten years, she had a mature grasp of scriptures and had memorized a fair amount. Additionally, she almost never spent any time in the living room. I knew that she would infer that the meeting with me wasn't to socialize.

In the living room, I asked her to find certain verses and explain them. In James she read of the tongue, Ephesians was about not letting unwholesome words out, and Romans warned against causing your brother to stumble.

After she simply explained each verse, I asked quietly, "Do you remember what you and your friend were talking about in the car today?"

She looked chagrined. I asked her what she should do. She hesitated, then said, "Tell God I'm sorry."

I told her that it was a good idea. Then I asked if there was anything else. "Tell you I'm sorry."

"That's good," I said. "Anything else?"

She paused and thought a moment, then said, "Tell my friend I was wrong."

I was a teacher. But because I had changed and done my work, Alice had become my teacher's aide. She taught herself that evening. It was a pleasure to listen to what she had learned, and our warm bond was unbroken as the lesson was learned.

The little one in your home is growing into something new. If you are also growing and changing into something new, you can show the kid how it's done. A scripture that helps is, "Let no unwholesome word proceed from your mouth, but only such a word as is good for edification and according to the need of the moment, so that it will give grace to the hearer" (Ephesians 4:29). *Edification* is the *building up* of a dwelling place—or in this case, raising up a child into a mature adult.

They become like us.

The Mystery of Teachableness

I use the term *teachableness* to describe the inclination of a person to receive instruction. Being teachable is a condition of being receptive to teaching. It is certainly enhanced by a good attitude toward the teacher, but it is not exactly an attitude. There are virtues that promote an openness to education, but teachableness itself seems to be more than a virtue.

Being aware that I do not possess all wisdom and that you could possibly teach me something new, along with a confession that I could be blind to certain truths, is a foundation of being teachable. To philosophers and psychologists, teachableness is an expression of *intellectual humility*, a virtue of people who have a capacity for honest self-examination.

Theologically, being teachable is a manifestation of the spiritual fruit of *gentleness*, a glad submission with a willingness to be *guided* (led and taught). Wisdom, the curriculum for child-rearing, is particularly available for the humble who believe that any of us—parent, child, you, me—any of us could learn from any of the others.

God knows the mystery of the human heart, the spirit of contriteness, and the feeling of regret that renders a person teachable in a moment of repentance and reconciliation. In scripture, being teachable is often related to being contrite. David sang:

> Do not remember the sins of my youth or my transgressions; according to Your lovingkindness, remember me, for Your goodness' sake, O Lord. Good and upright is the Lord; therefore He instructs sinners in the way. He leads the humble in justice, and He teaches the humble His way. (Psalm 25:7–9)

Because being teachable is so mercurial in children, parents who can consistently teach have learned to gauge the teachableness of their children in a moment or circumstance before teaching is attempted. The principle is, "When your child is in a teachable moment, teach; when your child is not teachable, nurture and/or wait until he is teachable, then teach."

The vigilance required for this skill must be coupled with reticence, a conservation of words. The parent who is *talking too much* is the outstanding reason for the child who is *not listening*. I learned this at work, then I experimented with my own children. I learned that by only speaking directions in a golden moment, I could get jobs done without confrontations. Meanwhile, I practiced reticence so that I did not inadvertently offer the children practices in *not listening*.

When Julie was very young, I realized that she emotionally processed my excess of words as comfort. What I would consider as *reasoning* (usually answering her question of "Why?") actually seemed to encourage her defiance. I spoke to my wife about this, and we decided that together, we would train ourselves in reticence.

Soon we developed a secret way of signaling when one of us was talking too much. The signal was a hand over the mouth or an index finger signing a slit to the throat. We agreed to be grateful for the help and not take offense if one of us was stuck in an ineffective argument with Julie, and the other signaled to knock it off.

When Julie was a two-year-old with a growing vocabulary, I used words I knew she understood to subtly redirect her or to help her prepare to obey. Meanwhile, when things were good, I would nurture her with lots of conversation, so she would remember the moments of life we enjoyed together. I also modeled the rudiments of apology and forgiveness by admitting my own mistakes with her in conversation. I was pretty sure that she understood the *feeling* of a contrite spirit by this time.

Julie was a little more than two years old when, at the supper table, she sized me up and basically spewed a deliberately offensive challenge at me. I must have stimulated this insolence by some stupid demand. (By then I knew she was strong-willed and that her general policy was to resist my authority.)

I said, "Honey, you can't talk that way to Daddy. Go to your room until you can tell me you're sorry."

That was fine with her. She left with a "Humph!" and slammed her bedroom door shut.

A few hours later, it was bedtime. I spoke to her from the doorway. "Julie," I said. "Are you sorry for the way you talked to me?"

Lying on top of her bedcovers and staring at the ceiling with arms folded and her little chin thrust out, she responded, "Nope."

"Well, it's bedtime, and I'm going to bed. Let me know when you're sorry." I shut the door as I walked away.

That wasn't the way she usually went off to sleep. Bedtime was a highlight of her day, with an hour or more of the two of us reading books, playing with toys, telling stories, and singing songs. But I knew her attitude was against me by her posture and conversation, and I did not want to encourage a bad attitude further by my presence. That night, I privately prayed for her and for the restoration of our relationship. It was a long night for me.

The next morning, I called to her from the doorway again. "Julie." She looked up sleepily at me. "Do you remember what you said to me last night?"

By the gradual light on her face, I could tell that she remembered. "You still must tell me you're sorry."

Then, as I shut the door between us again, I said, "Please don't come out of your room until you can do that." Fifteen minutes later, she was in my arms, in tears, and it was over—at least for that moment.

It wasn't too many days later that she challenged me again at the supper table, followed again by the trundling off to her room, the slamming of the door, and then to bed without so much as a "Good night." But this time, just after midnight, she came to me and woke me up. In tears, she told me she was sorry.

I guess she had learned that if I said it, I meant it, and the middle of the night is scary when you're two years old and not sure where your daddy is. She also learned that Daddy could and would wait for her to change her bad attitude and would always forgive. As the years passed, her bedroom had become her blacksmith shop, a workspace to bang out the dents when her bent attitude needed repair. Looking back, her midnight confession was a milestone in our relationship.

Meanwhile, I learned that Julie was always teachable when she was sorry and that I could wait longer than she could. Teachableness remained a mystery—it is still a mystery to me—but it is related to humility and a contrite spirit. These are wonderful mysteries as well.

Submission and Teachableness

In teaching seminars with parents, I sometimes used a set of four different sketches of a horse. In one, the horse was wild and free on a hilltop, the wind blowing its mane. In another image, the horse was in a corral, a bridle on its muzzle and a cowboy standing, braced with the reins in hand. A third showed the cowboy riding the violently bucking bronco in the corral. In a fourth sketch, the cowboy was in the saddle, and the two were a team, working together as they herded steers. The two were at last fulfilling their purpose in life.

A set of these four pictures was for each parent in the seminar. I instructed them to consider the horse as their child and to arrange them in a logical sequence. I hoped that they would see the free mustang on the hill as the beginning and the well-trained work horse as the final product. But in each group, some parents would place the wild stallion at the end of the four images as the result of the story. Rather than seeing their children as undisciplined and beyond authority at the start, they thought of them as having a destiny of proud autonomy, rising beyond the restrictions of authority.

Parents worry about many things. One of the worries is about the way the child sees himself and the development of *self-esteem*. Parental encouragement and consolation are proper and necessary. But if they are not well distinguished from indulgence, spoiling, false praise, and jive in the name of "building self-esteem," they can be the root cause of the older child's arrogance, his final rejection of his parents, and then estrangement from God, like a wild stallion on a hill.

A foal born in the wild is driven by biological urges but is unaware of being under authority. By all external observations, it seems to be free. But in the beginning, the young horse is helpless and needy. As it struggles to stand, then staggers toward its mother, its biological demands are quickly tended by the mare. Like any newborn, the foal has a natural willfulness. Without an awareness of propriety or a care for the imposition, it insists that its interests be served. So who is making demands, and who is responding? Who is in charge?

Surely this is a parallel to the newborn infant. Only a parent under the healthy influence of oxytocin would repeatedly submit to the narcissistic, moment-to-moment demands of a newborn. It's not that the baby is aware of his behavior. He is not *thinking* he is superior. He is just *acting* as if it is true. Meanwhile, the parent's response seems to confirm his superior status. If this misapprehension of superior status is not effectively modified, the toddler will likely continue to contend for a superior status.

If humility is the virtue of maintaining a low status relative to others, children are unaware of their humility for years. Meanwhile, by our doting complicity, the evidence grows that their status is superior each time their demands are met. The selfish view of toddlers and their presumption of a superior status seems to contradict the teaching of Jesus when He featured a child as an example of humility: "He called a child to Himself and set him before them, and said, 'Unless you are converted and become like children, you will not enter the kingdom of heaven. Whoever then humbles himself as this child, he is the greatest in the kingdom of heaven'" (Matthew 18:2–4).

That little guy's parents must have been proud. They probably spoke with all of their friends of this moment. Jesus Himself had said it: "*Our* child is the *greatest.*" As the child listened to his parents gush, he may have concluded that he must be something really special. The kid may even have proudly thought he was more humble than any other person in the kingdom. That's the way it is in modern, professionally approved, child-rearing land. The parents treasure the children and encourage them in their self-esteem (which is, of course, entirely appropriate). Then, in innocence, the children assume they have superior status and challenge those in proper authority.

So Jesus endorsed the humility of a child that day, and the disciples were caught off guard. The teaching is counterintuitive, and initially, I was perplexed as I encountered countless little ones and wondered what the humility of a child might be.

Humility is usually framed as a virtue. It is the deliberate, thoughtful, and possibly costly lowering of status that makes humility a virtue. Given the wisdom of certain other verses about the nature of children, it was clear that the humility of Jesus's teaching was not referring to a child's intentionally assuming a low status by his own sacrifice.

With contemporary official agencies like the US Congress and the UN promoting the rights of children, many adults being suspicious of authority in general, and the decline of manners in society, many parents now lack the confidence to be in charge. Someday, their children who are immunized to humility because of fawning praise may permit certain chosen ones like college professors to teach them. And they may listen. But their understanding will be contaminated if a false sense of superiority is reinforced by hours of teaching. Paul wrote of this eventual consequence of recklessly praising the immature as their knowledge grows: "We know that we all have knowledge. Knowledge makes arrogant" (1 Corinthians 8:1).

Normal, healthy children move toward adulthood with increasing knowledge and self-determination. In maturity they may properly make independent decisions that oppose the will of their parents, applying their own life principles to their circumstances. Before this time, though, they need information, leadership, training, and guidance. All of these needs require submission and acceptance of teaching. Without the instruction of wisdom, they may fail to discern false or evil authority someday.

From the perspective of the cowboy in the four sketches, bringing the horse under authority in the corral pays off in consistency of both performance and fellowship. Similarly, if your little one learns wisdom from you and if he is of reliable service in the family that cherishes him and wants the best for him, it will be the result of your authority being finally established.

Consistently submitting to your authority is his best hope for learning to cope in adult society and to find the fulfillment of his dreams and goals. It is also his best hope for learning the fear of the

Lord and someday learning God's purpose for his life. If he walks in wisdom because of your input, it will be the result of your authority being finally established. From the perspective of the cowboy, decisively bringing the horse under authority in the corral pays off in consistent performance, fellowship, and final outcome.

Humility is deliberately lowering yourself.

Humility and Teachableness

O f all the virtues waiting for your child to learn, humility is probably most associated with being teachable. Significantly, I wasn't conscious of the importance of this virtue for children when I was rearing my own, and I can't recall any parent asking about how to teach humility. Maybe this is because it seems counterintuitive with children. We control their welfare and direct their lives. From an adult perspective, they have no status, so there is no need.

The virtue of humility is not merely a result of life circumstances in which a person is forced into a subordinate role. It is an intentional lowering of status relative to others for the purpose of servanthood. The virtue is based on a fundamental decision to submit and then to practice the vigilance and self-control required to remain in submission.

The practice of humility begins with an honest effort to put the welfare of others ahead of self and do so with a *good attitude*. It does not imply a lowered self-esteem but does include an accurate, private evaluation of self-worth as it refuses (or repents of) negative thoughts of self and others.

Because of our self-awareness, our private evaluations of others (especially opinions, judgments, and prejudices), and our lack of consistency in good manners, the practice of humility is uneven for most of us. Our children are likely to learn an inconsistency in attitude from us.

Scientific information on the developing brain indicates that toddlers apparently don't contemplate themselves much. Years must pass before they could really *know* that their submission to your direction is actually the will of God, and because of that, they should altruistically place your priorities above their own (Ephesians 6:1). In the meantime, if they are teachable, they can learn the practices of humility such as consistent listening, and you can teach and model the wisdom of humility as a valuable virtue.

When Jesus distinguished the humility of a child, He was admiring the child's *acceptance* of his dependent state, not his self-perception and conscious determination to maintain his lowly status. The humble are the "poor in spirit," who have nothing (Matthew 5:3). A young child's dependency on being provided with each and every necessity is the condition of humans who humbly accept the reign of God and find that the wealth of His kingdom is theirs.

All children begin life in this totally impoverished state. Then they begin to accumulate things, take their entitlements for granted, and learn to say "Mine." As they assert themselves and choose the way they want to go, rather than submit and gratefully accept the best way, they begin solving the problems of life by their own methods. When these solutions are not based on biblical wisdom, they can become the practiced habits of dysfunctional coping. If the child learns to maintain the humble status of being teachable, he can learn effective, healthy coping.

A common example of coping is thumb-sucking, an important early developmental milestone for a young infant. Thumb-sucking is understood as a self-taught solution for the stress of loneliness, a sign of the baby's relieving the unpleasant feelings of isolation by his own initiative. This discovery of a solution for feelings of stress is healthy *coping* at first, but after a while, it is no longer an appropriate solution for the stress of loneliness. Most children lay aside this habit as they become aware of other solutions, such as socializing with peers.

It is common for parents (and dentists) to be concerned about three- or four-year-olds still thumb-sucking. Commonly, others directly disparage these children and their "bad" habit. As the children continue this means of coping into school years, they learn shame and experience the added stress of poor self-esteem. But if they aren't teachable, they don't learn to practice the skills and social manners of friendship, which are a better solution for the stressful feelings of loneliness. So they soothe their lonely feelings in the same old way, reenforcing the habit and increasing their guilt and low self-esteem.

I sucked my thumb until school age; by that time, I was doing it only in my bed at night. I don't remember my parents ever commenting on the issue, although my older brother offered his opinion periodically. I do remember stopping the habit.

One day, I had enough awareness of my childish habit to say to my mother, "I wish I didn't suck my thumb."

"Would you like for me to help?" she asked.

With the unintentional humility of a child, I told her, "Yes."

"Okay. Every morning that you wake up with a wet thumb, I will give your older brother a penny." He got one penny the next day, and I no longer sucked my thumb. I also *felt* better by overcoming my dysfunctional coping.

If you are a parent, you are a teacher. It is a huge advantage to be a teacher of a child who is reliably teachable. But for your child to be reliably and consistently teachable, he must first consistently submit to your authority. In order to remain submissive with a good attitude, he must learn and practice the virtue of humility, that is, cheerful submission based on his proper, lower status. It remains with you to distinguish for him this lower status from his value to you, which is far beyond measure.

I don't think that my parents intentionally taught me humility. My memories of childhood are warm and comforting as I consider the self-deprecating humor of my father and the good cheer of my mother. They both followed the rules and accepted authority in their world of which I was aware. Without meddling or scrutinizing, they assumed I would likewise do my best as a servant, and they seemed to appreciate my efforts. They also assumed I would listen. I don't remember ever questioning whether or not I should, and they were always on the teacher's side when issues at school arose.

They both encouraged and consoled me, and each spoke highly of the other. Neither elevated themselves in my presence, but I don't remember considering that they were anything other than my united superiors. From this foundation, I became more reliably teachable.

I don't remember being consciously aware of submission until I was a freshman in college. But by then, I was a trained disciple who could receive instruction without resistance. The stress of the plebe system at The Citadel was like a branding iron that sealed my position as a willing learner who was ready to submit for the next lesson, including warming up a toilet seat.

Life is like this. Sooner or later, most of us are humbled by the unfolding events of our lives. Meanwhile, as parents, we must pay attention to ourselves and to our teaching (see 1 Timothy 4:16).

Developing a Teachable Heart

S ome people seem inclined to receive teaching most of the time. By their eagerness (or seriousness), they seem to just be asking for a teacher to get started. In a familiar Bible story, the Lord introduced a teacher named Philip to such a person on a desert journey. The man was rocking along in his chariot, reading scripture, when Philip recognized and seized the teachable moment.

"Philip ran up and heard him reading Isaiah the prophet, and said, 'Do you understand what you are reading?' And he said, 'Well, how could I, unless someone guides me?' And he invited Philip to come up and sit with him" (Acts 8:30–31). The Greek word translated as *guide* renders both *lead* and *teach*. The moment was a highlight in the dream of every thoughtful parent as Philip easily scored a touchdown with a lesson.

Theologically, when you became a Christian, the Holy Spirit entered your life and became your live-in teacher. He is a wise and powerful roommate who can not only influence you far beyond your capacities to naturally grasp wisdom but can also help you become teachable. Jesus said that "when He, the Spirit of truth, comes, He will guide you into all the truth... He will take of Mine and disclose it to you" (John 16:13–14).

Years later, the apostle John wrote that through the Holy Spirit, "the anointing which you received abides in you, and you have no need for anyone to teach you; but as His anointing teaches you about all things, and is true and is not a lie, and just as it has taught you, you abide in Him" (1 John 2:27).

Yet many Christian parents who have the Holy Spirit within seem anxious, alarmed, and befuddled about the will of God and the way of wisdom. The reason may be related to a failure to consistently abide in Him. Abiding is a continuous, close association with the teacher who is always ready to teach. His influence is part of the mystery of being teachable. With kindness and dignity, He leads you to practice vigilance and to listen. When you resist, He doesn't yell or nag. He waits until you are ready, then He teaches.

Jesus, the master teacher, regularly dealt with people who either were, or were not, in a teachable state. He was always quick to first establish His teaching authority. Then He would often engage those He was teaching through enigmatic parables or with preparatory questions and directions to help them receive His teaching.

Jesus often tested for teachableness before presenting a lesson. An example was during a supper in the courtyard of Simon the Pharisee (Luke 7:36–49) when a woman Simon knew to be a *sinner* entered the dining area and began washing the feet of Jesus. Simon did not speak, but Jesus recognized his host's *attitude* and said, "'Simon, I have something to say to you.' And he replied, 'Say it, Teacher'" (Luke 7:40). A paraphrase might read, "Simon, if you would like to learn something, I have something for you. Please let me know if you will listen before I go further." And Simon's reply might read, "I recognize you as 'teacher' and I am listening."

The wise teacher knows that even by this concession of teaching authority, the person being offered the lesson may not like what he is about to hear and may reject the teaching. But Simon's answer was a beginning that would make a teacher hopeful. Ultimately, the passage does not clarify Simon's reaction to the teaching, but still, Jesus did impart the lesson with Simon's conscious agreement to listen.

A far different story of a teachable moment occurred when Jesus spoke to Saul after knocking the man off his horse. Saul took his Hebrew heritage seriously and had devoted his life to the study of scripture. He was earnestly living his life before God as a teacher but did not realize that he was actually not teachable.

Saul's lack of *intellectual humility* closed his mind to the fresh wisdom introduced in the teaching of Jesus, so he failed to learn God's great purpose for mankind. Then, "as he was traveling, it happened that he was approaching Damascus, and suddenly a light from heaven flashed around him and he fell to the ground. A voice said to him, 'Saul, Saul, why are you persecuting Me?'" (Acts 9:3–4).

Years later, Saul retold the story by the authority of his new name and status as the apostle Paul. He recalled that when the Lord asked the question, He had revealed to Saul something about his own unteachable state: "It is hard for you to kick against the goads" (Acts 26:14). Goads are sharp pointed sticks used to move unwilling oxen along in front of a plow. If an ox refuses to go ahead and so kicks backward, the *prick* from behind reminds him to keep going the right way.

It is true that any of us, regardless of how far we've gone in formal education, are occasionally not willing to listen to a teaching. It is a tragedy that many of us seem to hold to a life policy of resisting teaching we don't like as we "kick against the goads." This policy of being unteachable can begin very early in life and can be the root cause of daily conflicts in the home for years. When not being teachable is associated with not being contrite, it can darken a whole lifetime of relationships.

If you recognize in your child a spirit of resistance to teaching, it would be wisdom to "test the spirit" before you speak a point of instruction. A conversation might sound like this:

"I want to tell you something about that. Are you listening?"

"What do you want to say?"

"I will tell you when you agree to listen."

If there is no agreement at this point from a child who may be unteachable, now you know that the clown with the pie may be coming next and so, proceed with caution.

Not being teachable is a condition of the heart, and the Creator of hearts intends to provide the ultimate answer: "I will give you a new heart and put a new spirit within you" (Ezekiel 36:26). Meanwhile, parents who want to reach hearts that are, at best, unevenly teachable, should remember that "the words of wise men are like goads" (Ecclesiastes 12:11). Here, the words of the wise are spoken in the right moment into the good soil of the parable of the sower. "The seed in the good soil, these are the ones who have heard the word in an honest and good heart, and hold it fast, and bear fruit with perseverance" (Luke 8:15).

True Christian conversion and the indwelling of the Holy Spirit is a surpassing advantage in the life of your child. Meanwhile, the condition of being teachable remains an enduring mystery. Your prayer as a loving parent is for your child's heart to be changed by the Creator of hearts. Your hope for your child is "Today, if you hear His voice, do not harden your hearts, as in the rebellion" (Hebrews 3:15 ESV). Your practice with your child is, "I say it; you do it."

Coping and Enduring

I often discussed with parents how to effectively change the behavior of preschool children who lived in messy bedrooms. The slums were extensive; so was the nagging. Christmas presents only added to the problem. A typical conversation might have been:

"Toby gets books and toys out and then doesn't put them back. Sometimes I can't even push his door open because of all the junk."

"How many of the items does he regularly play with or use?"

"Only a few. The rest just seem to pile up under the bed and on the floor. Then they stay there until I finally get serious with him."

"What does it mean to 'get serious'?"

"I yell loud enough and tell him I will not tolerate the mess anymore."

"And then...?"

"The next day, it's a mess again. And I start nagging again."

"So I guess you *do* tolerate it. What does Toby say about all of this?"

"Sometimes he cries and complains that there's too much to pick up."

"Do you ever help him pick up?"

"When guests are coming over, the room is halfway decent because I went in there and straightened up."

In this exhausting, daily drama of great emotion, a mother who said she would not tolerate her child's mess was, in fact, tolerating it. (Her nagging is plain evidence of tolerating.) She was also enabling him when she lowered her standard and fixed the issue herself. Her child, meanwhile, was learning improper conversation, codependency, and dysfunctional coping.

Coping is basically taking an action to relieve the uncomfortable feelings of stress. Toby felt overwhelmed by the mound of stuff awaiting his inadequate attention. The chemically driven emotions of his stress neutralized him, even as his mother was feeling the effects of her own stress chemicals that drove her to nag. When her cork predictably blew, she then modeled to her child the improper conversation and dysfunctional coping he would further learn to practice.

Feelings of stress can be alarming, especially to children. They whine, cry, or even *lose it* because of circulating chemicals. For years, they do not consciously recognize their anxiety; they just experience their chemically charged feelings and go where the feelings take them. Eventually, the bad feelings can become the dominant issue, beyond the original cause of the stress.

Toddlers refuse to let mothers out of their sight because of the effect of chemicals. Entirely healthy school-aged children complain of daily stomachaches with no physical or laboratory evidence of illness because of normal but disturbing inner chemical actions.

Because children are dependent, mostly without resources of their own, and innocent about finding effective, healthy solutions for their problems, they often enlist allies as part of their coping. The most available ally for most children is a well-intentioned and even smart parent. Parents unwittingly become victims of manipulation by their children who can be remarkably creative in their efforts to cope.

For instance, I once knew a smart, sleep-disturbed preschooler with precocious language development who frequently complained of being *bored*. He had rationally convinced his mother to prepare two full breakfasts for him each twenty-four hours.

"Is that okay?" she asked.

"I don't know," I mused. "What's in a breakfast?"

"Oh, vegetable omelets, toast, milk, cereal with fruit, pancakes, bacon, the works."

"Sounds like a pretty good diet. When are the two breakfasts served?"

"At 7:00 a.m. and 2:00 a.m.," she said.

"Does that fit into your schedule?"

"Well, I have to get up at one in the morning to prepare the two o'clock breakfast."

In this case, a child who was precocious in language development (but not in mature reasoning) had talked his mother into becoming a codependent enabler. The actual issue was that the child was lying awake in the night, and boredom was producing stress chemicals that demanded a solution. Mother was fun at 2:00 a.m., and she served refreshments.

The contagious nature of stress in a close relationship was apparent in this case. Her own feelings of anxiety had compelled her to overrule her good judgment, lower her standards, and then model dysfunctional coping as the chef of the Anytime Breakfast Bar.

If the issue that brings on dysfunctional coping can be eliminated, it should be. A thumb will stay out of a mouth with a harmless dental appliance; stuff that will not be missed from a disordered room can be gradually and discretely removed before the neighbors call the police. Also, whether or not there is a final solution for your child's issue, it is important that you practice vigilance in recognizing and dealing with your own feelings of stress.

Enduring rather than coping seems to be the activity encouraged in scriptures for stressful conditions. Enduring (or *persevering*) does not remove a memory, overcome a circumstance, or fix a person. It is an inward activity of building character and standing firmly in the face of difficulties by meditation, prayer, and Bible study. Enduring is a virtue developed by practicing other virtues such as vigilance, patience, and self-control.

Delivering children from dysfunctional coping and helping them understand and express their feelings of stress in a healthy way is hard but good work. It is a job best done by wise parents with a firm grip on biblical wisdom and self-control in their conversation.

Success is for those who are being transformed by renewed minds (Romans 12:2). It is for those who understand their own feelings and "because of practice, have their senses trained to discern good and evil" (Hebrews 5:14).

The Contrite Heart

When Jesus said that "a disciple is not above his teacher" (Matthew 10:24), He was speaking of the relative difference in status between the teacher and student. Imparting a lesson requires submission. A disciple who is "above his teacher" is an individual who will not learn from his teacher because of a bad attitude. In that moment, such a person is not truly a disciple.

Many behavioral therapists advise *time-out* in order to modify the behavior of a child who elevates his status and refuses to listen. In psychological theory, this time alone provides an opportunity to recover emotional control and agree to submission.

An example is a three-year-old who, in the midst of a bad day, finally crosses the line, committing some time-out-worthy offense. He is banished to his room until his temper tantrum is concluded and then remains isolated for three additional minutes, a minute for each of his years. At the conclusion of the exercise, the parent then approaches the child (or the child asks if he can return), and the misbehavior is analyzed in a calm discussion. Presumably the discussion concludes with the child's agreement to improve his conduct, and all live happily ever after—until he blows it again because he has not changed his attitude and remains convinced that he is "above" his teacher.

It is certainly sensible to train a child who has collapsed under stress to regain his composure in private. But do the added extra minutes of isolation result in reflection and self-examination? Are they understood to be a discipline or a punishment? Is it reasonable to assume that a three-year-old, who only a few minutes earlier was standing defiantly against his parent's authority, has rationally concluded because a few minutes have passed that his parent is right after

126

all and that he must now let his parent be in charge? What lesson has he actually learned?

If children are morally neutral and if their periodic rejection of parental authority is accepted as a healthy expression of immature autonomy, then we need only to modify their behavior and give them time to think about it. But if the Bible is correct and their willfulness is an expression of foolishness or a crooked intent of the heart, then we might understand isolation in a completely different light.

Instances of time-out are prominent in the Bible. But unlike psychological theory, they seem to provoke strong emotions, not relieve them. Consider Jonah and his time-out experience: "All Your breakers passed over me. So I said, 'I have been cast out of your sight'…while I was fainting away, I remembered the Lord" (Jonah 2:3–7). Now consider the nation of Israel, the child of God, in exile: "By the rivers of Babylon, there we sat down and wept when we remembered Zion" (Psalm 137:1).

The Father of the nation of Israel used isolation as a child-rearing technique but not as a means of behavior modification. The disobedience of His child was not a behavioral problem in His eyes. Rather, it was evidence of a much more ominous problem. Israel went into exile because of resistance to the Father's authority—an issue of attitude, not behavior.

The prophets clarified the Father's reason for sending His "sons" to their room:

> Listen, O heavens, and hear, O earth; for the Lord speaks, "Sons I have reared up but they have revolted against Me." (Isaiah 1:2)

> Say now to the rebellious house, "Do you not know what these things mean?" Say, "Behold, the king of Babylon came to Jerusalem, took its king and princes and brought them to him in Babylon." (Ezekiel 17:12)

Willful disobedience was proof that the hearts of God's children were misaligned and opposed to the Father's teachings because they had elevated their status above His. God responded to their rebellion with exile. He anticipated that the stress of isolation and the loss of fellowship would convert their hearts, bring their hearts back into proper alignment, and make their hearts teachable.

When the divine Father places His child in isolation, it is not time-limited. Time-out continues until its end is achieved.

> I will give them one heart and put a new spirit within them. And I will take the heart of stone out of their flesh and give them a heart of flesh, that they may walk in My statutes and keep My ordinances and do them. Then they will be My people and I shall be their God. (Ezekiel 11:19–20)

The fruit of isolation—a conversion in the spirit—occurs throughout the Bible by the will of God. From the exile to the prodigal, repentance and restoration are always the goal. Isolation is one of the greatest stresses of the human experience. As the walls close in, solitude fosters the pressure of boredom, the oppression of loneliness, and the frustration of an inability to express will. In the end, the unpleasant feelings of isolation can force a change of heart.

Children often do not endure isolation well. This is especially the case if we have taken the time to build meaningful fellowship into our relationship. The loss of a rich relationship then becomes the pivot point for realignment.

We may suffer while they are in isolation, but the rebellion was their choice, so the responsibility for repentance is also theirs. How the human heart changes is a mystery, but our Father has given us the privilege to participate in the miracle of realigning our children's hearts, if we can believe. When the length of time of isolation is determined, not by the age of our child but rather by his contriteness, with sincere regret and recommitment, there is a realistic hope that a proper alignment can be restored. Once again, our child can be our disciple who listens and who is ready to practice going the right way.

A classic Bible story of a contrite heart producing a teachable spirit is of King David after his adulterous encounter with Bathsheba (2 Samuel 11–12). After their affair, David may have still been on the throne, but in a real, spiritual way, God placed him in isolation.

The king was feeling the effects of the chemicals of anxiety when he wrote, "When I kept silent about my sin, my body wasted away through my groaning all day long. For day and night Your hand was heavy upon me; my vitality was drained away with the fever heat of summer" (Psalm 32:3–4). In isolation, there was only silence from the Father of Israel.

David was feeling the distress of guilt in his isolation, but importantly, his confidence in God's love kept him from shame. He knew that in Hebrew law, his only hope for relief from his guilt was the forgiveness of God.

In faith, he returned, and in a contrite spirit, asked for the mercy he knew would come because the God of Israel was merciful. "I said, 'I will confess my transgressions to the Lord,' and You forgave the guilt of my sin… You are my hiding place; You preserve me from trouble; You surround me with songs of deliverance" (Psalm 32:5, 7).

A contrite confession and true forgiveness can lead to full reconciliation and growth of character. A child who is well bonded with his parent actually feels distress because of the pain he brought into his parent's life. When he is truly sorry and forgiven, his stress is relieved, and his apology can render him teachable for a fresh teaching of compassion.

The Great Commandment
for Children

When Jesus was asked which of the commandments was the most important, He answered, "'You shall love the Lord your God with all your heart, and with all your soul, and with all your mind'" Then He taught further, saying, "'The second is like it; 'You shall love your neighbor as yourself'" (Matthew 22:36–39). By the wisdom of Christ, the first rule necessarily includes the next; there is not the one without the other.

This principle is a helpful way to understand the first lesson of child-rearing: "When I say it, you do it." The child is still learning and practicing, so mistakes are inevitable. Therefore, the first lesson must be coupled with the second: "When you make a mistake, confess it and then listen again."

I learned these two inseparable principles early and confirmed them regularly through my forty years of pediatric practice. My professional days were sometimes quiet and sometimes hectic; occasionally, they were desperate. But only once do I recall thinking that in just doing my work, I could die a violent death. This occurred in the presence of an angry father, who was bigger and older than I was, and his teenage son, who was near the end of his high school days and a new patient.

The father had put up with all he was going to take when he brought his boy to the doctor that day. The kid had worn out his parents at home, and now he was in major trouble at school. He had a long record of behavioral problems and academic failure and had been socially promoted more than once. He had experimented with drugs in middle school and was popular at weekend parties. The parents had been told that he was about to be expelled.

When I spoke with my patient privately, he seemed more anxious and frustrated than angry. The way he stumbled over words as he answered my questions led me to suspect that he had some learning or communication problem. But he had never been tested for these things, and this particular office encounter was not the time.

I asked about conversations in the home with his parents. He told me it was the same, night after night. "My mother complains about something or tells me that one of her friends heard something bad about me. I try to explain, and then my dad piles on. It always ends bad."

When the father reentered the room, he glared at his son and took a seat. As I was speaking of his son's point of view, he quickly dismissed it and said that he would never have gotten away with this kind of stuff when he was growing up. "My father would have just used the belt again," he muttered.

I was seated on my little stool between these two. Their chairs blocked my access to the closed door of the little examining room. They were both big and strong. At one point, as the tension between them mounted, they both stood and moved aggressively toward each other. They would have met except I was in between. That's when I remember thinking, *I could die right now.* Of course, I didn't die, and the moment passed.

On a follow-up visit, I tried to counsel the parents and recommended testing for their son. But they decided testing would serve no purpose this late in his education; they would raise him the way they were raised. Years later, I met my former patient in maturity.

He had eventually obtained a high school equivalency certificate but was still in a running battle of misfiring words with his parents. We developed an enduring friendship, and I worked intensively with him as a tutor in some college-level courses. I came to know that he had an important, undiagnosed communication disorder that should have been recognized before he started school. I also learned that he was sometimes almost overwhelmed by decisions that ordinarily would be fairly easily resolved through logic, education, and previous life experiences.

My friend's relationship with his parents was still sour into adulthood. When we began our adult association, he would often speak of the tension he still felt when he was with them. They still compared him unfavorably to his siblings and did not accept him.

As an adult, he struggled with poor self-esteem but always sincerely apologized for his mistakes. I asked him where he learned that skill. He said that he had learned it from the Bible and his pastor, not in his home. Then he told me that he had learned to consciously remind himself to practice humility so that he could learn. Without prompting, he added that he was learning freedom from guilt through humility, confession, and apology. I knew, though, that he still struggled with shame because of his childhood experiences.

Then I asked him a question, being fairly sure of the answer beforehand. "Do you remember your parents ever apologizing to you when you were young?"

"No...never."

The point of child-rearing is to bring a child to moral maturity. The process of maturation is, by definition, a process of change. Moral change occurs as new insight is gained and then folded into daily decisions and lifestyle. In all of this process, mistakes are inevitable.

For adults, daily moral decisions are often unconsciously predetermined by unstated policy. For example, "I am a married man, therefore, I don't do those things," is a fixed thought that determines automatic decisions.

But children are moving on to a new status called adulthood. Where they are going, they have never been before, and moral policies are yet to be established. Moral and behavioral decisions can be inconsistent as each child makes his own progress on the journey to maturity. Some never really arrive.

When a child makes a mistake, if he survives and realizes the mistake was made, he then must cope and carry on. If he is not instructed and practiced in a policy of confession and repentance, first modeled by his parent, he will likely learn only dysfunctional coping. If he does not offer a contrite apology, with feelings of sincere regret, he will not experience the dramatic contrast of joy and peace when he is forgiven. This is the danger of the insincere apology and skeptical forgiveness, which is commonly heard between a child and parent:

"Okay, I'm sorry. Whatever."

"Well, you don't sound sorry to me. You'd better not let me catch you doing that again!"

This is a good example of neither apology nor forgiveness. Children don't know to listen and to truly apologize unless they are taught it and practice it. The first commandment for children is "Listen." When you fail, the second is likewise: "Confess, and then listen again."

A contrite heart begins listening again.

PART 4

How You Feed a Cat

Our Father is not finished with us yet.

*Now we who are strong ought to bear the weakness of
those without strength and not just please ourselves.*

—*Romans 15:1*

*Brethren, if anyone is caught in any trespass, you who are
spiritual restore such a one in a spirit of gentleness; each one
looking to yourself, so that you, too, will not be tempted.*

—*Galatians 6:1*

Feeding a Cat

It's not difficult to feed a cat, assuming that you have an empty bowl, a bag of dry cat food, and a cooperative cat. All you need to do is take out the cat food, dump some in the bowl, put the bowl down near the cat, and return the unused cat food. People who live alone with their cats do it this way. They could do it in their sleep and sometimes probably do.

If you are a parent and have an obedient kid, there is another way to feed a cat. Given the conditions listed above, you say to your capable and compliant child, "Please feed the cat." This is even easier than feeding the cat yourself because the cat gets fed, and you continue to enjoy your child's company.

If you are a parent with a child who doesn't listen, there's still another way to feed a cat. You can tell *this* child to feed the cat, and let the drama unfold. This method seems to be preferred by many parents, even though relationships are strained and nothing useful occurs. It is also noisier and much less efficient. Its popularity persists, I suppose, because cats keep on needing to be fed, children enjoy practices in drama, and bad child-rearing habits are easier to keep than to break.

The basic problem of this method is that it unrealistically expects an unwilling child to be willing. *To be* willing is not the same as *to do* the work of feeding a cat. Dealing with what the child should *do* rather than correcting what the child should *be* only leads to the next skirmish over the cat bowl.

Doing is an expression of personality, which can, at some level, be measured. Because of this, doing can be assessed by scientific investigation and explanation. So behavior becomes an observable activity that psychologists and parents can evaluate and modify. (Your child plainly either does or doesn't feed the cat. This is something tangible and provable.)

On the other hand, *being* is an inner reality of the spirit. It is beyond a full and accurate appraisal of science and beyond the reach of someone on the outside to change. *Being* is about personhood—the self, the soul, the heart. *Being* is a concern of biblical wisdom, not of scientific speculation.

Biblical child-rearing deals with behavior, but more importantly, it presumes to address the issues of the child's heart. For instance, dishonor and bad attitudes are matters of the heart reflected in misbehavior.

A change of heart can bring about a change of behavior. But if the behavior is *modified* without a change of heart and the heart condition remains, the misbehavior is likely to return. This is why the father appeals in the scripture: "Give me your heart, my son, and let your eyes delight in my ways" (Proverbs 23:26). To the faithful Hebrew people, the Creator of their children was also the Father of their nation. As Father, He was seriously concerned about the hearts of "this people" who "draw near with their words, and honor Me with their lip service, but they remove their hearts far from Me" (Isaiah 29:13).

Christian parents, though, often confuse Hebrew and Christian theology concerning this God whom they are instructed to call "Father." They also often mistake Hebrew cultural child-rearing for the full revelation gleaned from incorporating principles of wisdom from both the Old and New Testaments.

Our Father offers Himself to be the example of a perfect parent. He makes understanding the inner personhood the focus of parental attention: "I, the Lord, search the heart, I test the mind, even to give to each man according to his ways" (Jeremiah 17:10). The prophet acknowledged this remarkably profound evaluation: "You know me, O Lord, you see me; and You examine my heart's attitude toward You" (Jeremiah 12:3).

Just as the perfect parent's judgment of His child's heart is accurate, Christian parents, by faith and their knowledge of their heavenly Father, can be assured that they have been given a divine capacity to judge the hearts of their own children. This capacity is the result of our faith, which holds as a basic principle that the divine person with all of His capacities actually lives within us.

As Christians, we are supposed to be conforming to the image of Christ by expressing the life of Christ in us. Presumably this is also an ideal a parent would hope for his child. Some years ago, many earnest Christians wore a wristband with the acronym WWJD. To the wearer, the band was a question that continuously asked, "What would Jesus do?" So what would Jesus do about feeding cats?

Jesus was such a humble servant that it is not difficult to guess that He would be the first to do it Himself. But among other important things, He was a teacher, focused on training His disciples and moving them to maturity. When His disciples had just returned in pairs after performing many miracles among the people and were then facing thousands of hungry people, He said something that sounds like a parent: "You give them something to eat!" (Mark 6:37). Of course, these were trained disciples who were well practiced in listening.

This is in contrast to a child who repeatedly fails to feed the cat when he is told. He doesn't need to practice *not* feeding the cat again. He needs to practice first-time obedience. If a mother or father were to ask me, "As a parent, how do you feed a cat?" I would rephrase the question, "How do you get your child to feed the cat by your command?" Now here's a question I can help resolve.

The parent who finds himself repeatedly saying "Feed the cat" with no good result does not need to keep on practicing giving meaningless commands. He needs to repent of his bad habit in conversation. Then he needs to practice certain virtues such as vigilance, patience, and self-control with an attitude of humility and a spirit of gentleness.

This is a difficult truth to face. We are fallen human beings and need help from the maker of children in our parenthood. Our true need is not to solve how you feed a cat; it is how I must change and become a more effective disciple—a learner being taught by the Holy Spirit within me.

The insight needed for change usually comes gradually. I know that it did for me, as I learned through experiences, trials, mistakes, and miraculous interventions. For God to accomplish His purpose— that the parent becomes conformed to the image of Christ—the parent first needs to change so that he can help his child to change. So now the final question is, "Why don't we consider these facts we know are true and change our ways?"

Learning about How You Feed a Cat

More than forty years ago, my own father was with me in a moment when my little girls needed some applied authority and a fatherly nudge. He observed that what I said and did was a little unusual but effective. So he asked, "Where did you learn that? It wasn't from me."

I told him that on Sundays I was teaching about God as the Father of Israel, and during the week, I was counseling parents and experimenting with his grandkids about what I was learning. He seemed amused.

Soon after that, I spoke with a grandmother in my practice who was a Bible teacher and an editor. She told me that what I was learning she had not heard before. She encouraged me to write what I was learning, even though I didn't think I had the time. I tried to write anyway.

I wrote and wrote, but I kept stalling because the information seemed too complex to express. Principles of theology, psychology, and child development were more tangled together than the vines rooting and running behind my garage. They were then knotted into unique counseling situations and endless wrinkles of individual personalities, circumstances, and my own life experiences with daughters who were continually growing and changing. Beyond this, my personal learning never stopped, and my understanding and interpretations grew with it.

I was aware fairly early that my divine Father was entrusting me with revelation. Then years later, I knew He was disciplining me: "For what son is there whom his father does not discipline? He disciplines us for our good, so that we may share His holiness" (Hebrews 12:7, 10). My discipline first became serious in military college, where I practiced severe self-control and developed a habit of self-inspection. Then in medical school, I learned to accept that my life was about others, not me, and that if I were to truly be a help, I would have to become competent in my professional work.

Now, many years later, I realize that what I was trying to put into words was actually the process of learning about how a cat might be fed by a parent's command. I suppose the years had to pass; more importantly, a lifetime was necessary for me to appreciate the patience of my heavenly Father. He was disciplining me as He had disciplined His children, thousands of years ago in the desert of Sinai.

The Father of Israel was "in the wilderness where you saw how the Lord your God carried you, just as a man carries his son, in all the way which you have walked until you came to this place... Thus you are to know in your heart that the Lord was disciplining you just as a man disciplines his son" (Deuteronomy 1:31; 8:5). This was the revelation I now appreciate personally: the Lord, my Father, has carried me and disciplined me.

I first spoke of God as the perfect parent in a large conference for pastors and physicians, using a passage from Malachi: "'A son honors his father and a servant his master. Then if I am a father, where is My honor? And if I am a master, where is My respect?' says the Lord of armies to you" (Malachi 1:6). It was a simple talk about the fundamental relationship issue between God and His stubborn child, Israel, and how the father's wisdom in the relationship determined the outcome for the child. It was a story that contained a second story with a bittersweet memory, ending with hope.

I spoke from a set of hand-drawn poster illustrations. In the first, a father with his child in his lap were sharing an ice cream cone. Next, they stood at a crossroads sign with two opposite choices. One arrow read "THE RIGHT WAY TO GO"; the other read "YOUR OWN WAY."

The intention of the father was that the child would walk with him along the right way to go. If the child would obey, the father would teach, the child would learn, and their fellowship would grow and never end. In this relationship of teacher and disciple, the child would understand his father's heart and learn to deeply regard him; that is, as time passed, he would learn to *honor* him.

Meanwhile, it was the father who would take the initiative and invest his time. He would be the one to establish authority and adjust to the reality that his child was innocent, apt to misstep, and inclined toward his own way. The father would have to be consistent and forgiving; he would also have to be resourceful, creative, and forward-thinking.

The first adjustments of the father in this walk along the right way necessarily highlighted the child's importance. The flowering of an intimate relationship and the child's receptiveness to discipleship teaching were a function of the father's humility. Paradoxically, the outcome of effective discipleship teaching was respect. Meanwhile, the child's success in going the right way would ultimately be a function of his obedience and submission.

In the next poster, the child was a disciple, sitting at the feet of his teacher. This was followed by a poster showing the father and child bonded within a big, outlined heart, walking hand in hand. This poster showed how it was supposed to be (and actually could be.)

Then I began a story within the story, using another poster. In this one, the father was pointing to "THE RIGHT WAY TO GO," but the willful child was choosing his own way, letting go of his father's hand as they parted. The pastors and physicians in the room reacted to the pathos and irony of the moment, many remembering, perhaps, their own childhoods or their own children's choices. Maybe some were thinking of a time when they parted company with their heavenly Father, choosing to go their own way. It was the moment in the garden for Adam and for the rest of us, sometimes, ever since.

The following poster was of the child alone, with the walls closing in on him. The stress of isolation and of his will being shut down was bitter and alarming. But somehow, perhaps the memory of his father's character and love would sweeten the loneliness with hope. (Without the prior fellowship, hope would have no foundation in fact.)

Then came a poster picturing the moment of confession and repentance. A person, childlike in size, was standing with his head bowed before a king on a throne. The king was clearly *in charge*, yet he also looked gentle and sympathetic as he considered a judgment. With forgiveness and full acceptance, the two resumed a teacher-disciple relationship. They walked off hand in hand on the right way to go—maybe, this time, endlessly.

The talk was simple but effective. The principles derived from references across the Old Testament were true for parents and children around the world, and it became the basis of a message I eventually taught from Africa to the Amazon to England to Beijing. I came to think of this everlasting story and its tragic story within as the set of instructions that come with each child for each parent, from the Creator of children. It is His Plan A and Plan B.

Plan A

1. As the Father of Israel, God dealt with Israel as a father, compassionately and righteously. His intention was to offer His child His teachings—*Torah*—and to enjoy fellowship on the right way to go (wisdom). "And I said, 'You shall call Me, My Father, and not turn away from following Me'" (Jeremiah 3:19).
2. If Israel valued the fellowship, listened to the teachings, and submitted to God's authority, the nation would be a disciple, a student (a learner) who is in fellowship with his teacher and is becoming like his teacher. *Discipline is training or practicing* doing it right. "Thus you are to know that the Lord your God was disciplining you just as a man disciplines his son" (Deuteronomy 8:5).
3. With a disciple's teachable spirit, Israel would continue to accompany his Father in an increasingly close fellowship and follow His teachings along the path of wisdom. "Your ears will hear a word behind you, 'This is the way, walk in it,'" whenever you turn to the right or to the left" (Isaiah 30:21).

'For I know the plans that I have for you,' declares the Lord, 'plans for welfare and not for calamity to give you a future and a hope.' (Jeremiah 29:11)

If Israel chose the right way to go, the nation would enjoy the companionship and discipline of God like a child with his father. This was Plan A.

Plan B

1. God is perfect, so He only goes the right way. When Israel chose to go its own way, which was frequently the case, the Father dealt with His child wisely, patiently, righteously, and faithfully, awaiting the inevitable results. Meanwhile, His child would learn the supreme value of fellowship and wisdom the hard way, through the stress of isolation in exile. "With the pure, You show Yourself pure, and with the crooked, You show Yourself astute" (Psalm 18:26).

2. The boredom, frustration, and loneliness of isolation would produce the stress necessary for a change of heart. The memories of fellowship would carry the hope of forgiveness. "For I am ready to fall, and my sorrow is continually before me. For I confess my iniquity; I am full of anxiety because of my sin" (Psalm 38:17–18).

3. Because of God's attractiveness as Father, the prophets knew that Israel in isolation would miss the fellowship and so would eventually regret, repent, and return to the rule of the perfect parent, sincerely confessing sin and gratefully receiving forgiveness. "But to this one I will look, to him who is humble and contrite of spirit, and who trembles at My word" (Isaiah 66:2).

According to their transgressions, I dealt with them.
(Ezekiel 39:24)

This was Plan B. After reconciliation and the restoration of fellowship, disciplining could resume, and the Father and child could follow Plan A, walking together along the right way to go.

PLAN A

"For I know the plans that I have for you," declares the Lord, "plans for your welfare...to give you a future."
—Jeremiah 29:11

"So choose life...by loving the Lord your God, by obeying His voice and by holding fast to Him."
—Deuteronomy 30:19-20

"And I said, 'you shall call Me, "My Father," and not turn away from following me.'"
—Jeremiah 3:19

Good Attitude

Honor

"I am Thy servant; give me understanding." —Psalm 119:125

PLAN B

"According to their transgressions, I dealt with them."
— Ezekiel 39:24

THE RIGHT WAY
YOUR OWN WAY

Bad Attitude

"All of us like sheep have gone astray, each of us has turned his own way."
—Isaiah 53:69

"Then they will know that I am the Lord their God because I made them go into exile." —Ezekiel 39:28

Teachable (Resume Plan A)

A Contrite Heart

"And I said, 'I will confess my transgressions to the Lord; and Thou didst forgive the guilt of my sin.'" —Psalm 32:5

Listening in Africa

I used to teach biblical child-rearing at international conferences in Africa. The pastors and other ministers attending the conferences were Bible-believing Christians but largely without formal theological training. A British friend first introduced me to this ministry. He was in Uganda, leading a discipleship group of pastors during the Rwanda genocide. The horror of seeing the Kagera River choked with the bodies of Rwandans killed by their Christian neighbors challenged his faith. He began a practice of personal repentance and teaching that Christians who are exhausted by living their lives like everyone else should repent and start over.

My friend and I came to know each other well in a discipleship group in America, where he heard me teach on the subject of "*love*." When I first accepted his invitation to teach the Bible in a large conference of pastors, I asked about preparations. He told me that "*love*" was the subject that needed to be taught, and I was already prepared.

Through him, I learned of the miserable social position most children in sub-Saharan Africa occupy. The AIDS epidemic had produced a growing number of orphans in cities. In Uganda, where the conferences were usually held, access to public education was limited, and most young children spent their days as unpaid laborers and water carriers.

By government policy and cultural norms, parental authority was almost absolute in the homes. When the children of Uganda failed to obey, they were often denied meals and physically abused. Commonly, a provoked parent would literally run a young child permanently out of the house. A local aunt or grandparent might accept such a child but often not. Banished and homeless, these children would then join the orphans on city street corners.

The pastors at the conferences, many of whom I came to know well, had been raised in this way. They thought it was "biblical," and they knew of no alternative. Those from nearby countries described similar experiences or worse. All over Africa, babies often were tenderly nursed; but then, as young children, they entered the workforce. In typical families, the children responded to adult rule like children everywhere. Some were submissive with a good attitude, some submitted but resented authority, and some overtly refused to obey.

Taking the time to train children in tasks was typically not done. They were simply told what to do, and when they failed, they were brutalized and/or discarded. In the towns and countryside, this devaluation of children was the norm. More tragically, the children were learning from their experiences, assuring that these dysfunctional traditions of child-rearing would pass to the next generation. I thought that the devaluation of children explained Rwanda.

The African pastors I taught seemed eager for change, and even outside of the conferences, Africans often seemed open to new ideas about dealing with children. For instance, during a long layover at the Nairobi airport, a young woman behind the counter of a gift shop was consistently welcoming to her customers. As the hours passed and I revisited her shop, we developed an intermittent conversation in English, which she spoke well. On one round, I picked up an item I had not seen previously. It was a wooden stick with a knob on one end, like a club, maybe sixteen inches long. It was covered with colorful beadwork; the knob had some shiny jewelry chain worked over it.

I asked, "What is this?"

"It is the Maasai chief's ruling stick," she replied.

"His ruling stick..." I mused. "How does it work?"

"It doesn't 'work.' He just holds it."

"Do you mean he doesn't beat the people with it?"

She laughed. "No. He holds it, and the people obey him." She was ready for the lesson.

"What is it called in your language?" I asked.

"It is *rungu*."

"*Rungu*... Have you ever heard the proverb, 'Spare the rod and spoil the child?'"

"Yes. Everyone in Africa knows that proverb."

"Do you know the Swahili word that translates the word *rod* in your Bible?"

"No," she replied.

"It's the same word that is in Psalm 23. 'Thy rod and Thy staff, they comfort me.' *Rungu* is the guiding stick of the shepherd and the scepter of the king."

Her eyes filled with tears. Then she said, "I wish my parents had known that."

As I taught in the conferences, I often recruited a child to demonstrate how to obtain obedience without noise and mayhem. (Children seemed to be everywhere.) After each teaching session, the assisting pastors would typically call on those listening to testify how they would change as parents in their own homes. The pastors would stand, one after another, and speak as parents of their own situations. Then they would frankly confess their failures and express their new intentions for change and for preaching the *new* message in their churches.

In one unforgettable moment of teaching, a woman pastor in my small group began to wail uncontrollably, so distraught that she couldn't speak. I was speaking through two interpreters and worried that I had caused some embarrassment. The next day, she seemed composed and joyful. I was still wary, but a pastor friend spoke to her in her language, then said to me, "The sister says she realized yesterday that she hates her children. Last night, she phoned them and asked them to forgive her. And they did!"

I was astounded. Her response to the new teaching was to confess and apologize. Then she returned to learn whatever came next, committed to doing it. She was a disciple who was listening and ready to practice the new way!

Teaching how you feed a cat in Africa would not be improved by adding advice to the old ways. Laying aside the old ways had to precede effective change. New wine would not work in old wineskins. "'Nor do people put new wine into old wineskins; otherwise, the wineskins burst, and the wine pours out and the wineskins are ruined; but they put the wine in fresh wineskins, and both are preserved'" (Matthew 9:17).

The old wineskin is a bag for the wine of bad habits we bring along with us into parenthood. When Christ is active in our lives, new understanding is new wine. Confession and repentance creates a fresh vessel for a new life as an enlightened and empowered parent.

Teaching American Parents
How You Feed a Cat

Teaching in Africa was a joy because the people in the conferences were so receptive. Beyond merely hearing, they also listened and followed through. I know this because on my repeated travels to rural Uganda, I collected written testimonies from the pastors and ministers. These documented dramatic changes in their own homes and revisions in their theological understanding as reflected in preaching and teaching in their churches. They also wrote of new and vibrant relationships with their children, whom they saw in a healthy light of respect.

I understood their listening and subsequent change to be a function of experiencing a true repentance before applying the lessons. The Africans I knew had become convinced of God's presence in their lives, and despite the disadvantages of their circumstances, they believed that God would deliver them.

On a cool evening in the mountains, I was on a red clay road, walking with a young woman who was the daughter of one of the pastors in my discipleship group. She was an elementary school teacher who seemed interested in the ideas I was presenting at the conference. I told her a story about walking on this road the previous evening. In the gathering darkness of yesterday, I vaguely saw a white object that seemed to be moving along slowly and irregularly. As I came nearer, I recognized that I was looking at a large plastic water can of the type carried by children throughout the area. Then I distinguished a second can at a different angle moving along with it.

Within a few yards, I realized the full picture. A child of about five years was dragging a water can through the mud by hand as he struggled forward with a second can on his back. He was bent so low to the ground that I could only see the cans. As I reached him, I realized that the second can was suspended from his forehead by a sling, and in the dark beside him was his brother, bigger and several years older. The little brother was dragging his big brother's water can through the mud; big brother was armed with a cane.

She and I then discussed authority in the classroom and ways of obtaining obedience without using physical coercion. As our paths separated, she said she was eager to meet with her children at school the next day.

"Why is that?" I asked.

"So that I can tell them I'm sorry and begin teaching a new way."

I was truly surprised at her answer but realized that it was the result of meetings like we were both attending together. The teaching regularly emphasized repentance, and the pastors were remarkably receptive to a message about changing their approach to child-rearing. Their prior repentance made my presentations relevant and effective as they began to consider cherishing the children and valuing them beyond their usefulness as workers.

It was in Africa that I first looked back at American parents I had counseled and realized how often they added aspects of things that I taught without discarding old interfering habits. For instance, they didn't seem to associate a need for repentance with excessive talking and ineffective commands. This resulted in layering new knowledge of retraining their children to listen on top of persisting bad habits of noise. The result was usually unsatisfactory.

Repentance produces authentic contact with God and miraculous change by His power. Without confronting the need for cleaning the slate by repenting, American parents were often confused by conflicting information from schools and experts and too many distractions and choices. Practically, many were unable to sense the reality of God's guidance in their lives. Without the divine insight and power made available by repentance, old ways still dominated.

A simple picture of this occurred in my life as I was waiting for a table in a local restaurant. Across from me was a young couple

I recognized from church, waiting for a table with their precocious three-year-old. I passively enjoyed the highly energized conversation between the mother and her daughter.

The little girl spoke to her mother with adult words and phrases, and the mother responded as adults might speak to adults, reasoning as though her child could also reason. When the mother occasionally corrected her child, the little one would refute or ignore what the mother had said. Then she would press ahead with her point of view. To my surprise, I became involved in this exchange when she seemed to size me up and boldly approach me. "You don't sit here," she said. Then pointing, she directed, "You sit over there."

I said, "I do?"

With a little lift of her eyebrows and a quick, regal nod of her head, she dismissed my doubt. The mother gently corrected her, then said to me, "I don't know where she learned that. We don't speak that way to her. We're trying to teach her good manners."

Actually, the mother was teaching her little girl to challenge her authority, and the child was demonstrating her skills of *not listening* as the mother practiced with her. I'm fairly sure that telling that particular little girl to feed a cat would stimulate a profound discussion and probably some drama; it would be of little use for a hungry cat.

If a moment like this had occurred in a Bible conference in Africa, I might have quietly asked permission, then engaged the mother in a teaching moment. Because of the remarkable teachableness of the people I met, I would then expect a pleasant and possibly life-changing conversation to follow.

But a busy restaurant in America was not the time and place to teach. More importantly, it was unlikely that the mother would have considered me to be her teacher or that she would see the implication of the difficult change in conversation I was recommending.

Receiving teaching requires a willing attitude, so I only nodded with a friendly smile and didn't speak my thoughts, which were, *Teaching is for people who listen. The teaching of good manners is for people who do not presume they are superior to the teacher.*

In Africa, an untrained child who was told to feed the cat would likely fail. Then he would be beaten, and if the cat was still around, it would have had to forage for itself. The same is true for cats across America.

If we don't confess the facts in front of us and change direction, one day our child will be well practiced in resisting authority and not listening but ignorant of the possibilities of change.

For American Christian parents, confession and repentance opens wide a new door of hope.

The Image of a Disciple

Some years ago, I did some time at Angola, the Louisiana State Penitentiary. Angola is the largest maximum-security facility in America. I was there by request to teach inmates known as the "Malachi Dads" how to be the teachers of their children who lived beyond the padlocks and razor wire.

The Malachi Dads were Christian fathers who would very likely not meet their children face-to-face for many years; some would never have a personal contact. Yet they loved them and wanted to somehow connect and fulfill their obligations. Their contacts would primarily be through letters, delivered to the care of guardians who were commonly hostile toward them.

Each time I entered a cellblock, I was thoroughly cleared by security officers. As I taught, I was frequently startled by whistles or alarms signaling spot security checks. In those moments, various men would excuse themselves for a few minutes, and I would remember that I was teaching convicted rapists and murderers.

The leaders of the Malachi Dads had earned seminary degrees as inmates. They were formally ordained by their denominations, and the warden considered them to be Christian missionaries. These gentle servants told me that they had to accept unrelenting scrutiny from their students as they quietly lived, taught, and counseled in their different cellblocks.

There was no escape from the judgment in the showers, in the exercise yard, or even on the cots at night. They knew they were distinguished among the inmates as Christian models and that their disciples were being influenced by the way they lived their lives. In the bright lights, noise, and interruptions, these leaders speculated with me about how to maintain teaching credibility under endless scrutiny and judgment.

In medical training, I formed opinions of those ahead of me and weighed what they were teaching with how they conducted themselves as physicians. In the end, as chief resident in pediatrics, I had become the one being judged by students and house staff. I did not attach significance to this until later, when I was teaching a verse from James: "Let not many of you become teachers, knowing that as such we will incur a stricter judgment" (James 3:1). It was when I connected this warning to the responsibilities of fatherhood that I first dealt with my own issues, specifically because I was the teacher of my little girls.

The stricter judgment of James's warning is undoubtedly a judgment of God. But in practical experience, teachers are open to judgment from just about everyone, particularly their students. Think of how you carried opinions of teachers who were part of your life and the way parents form opinions of schoolteachers whom their children talk about each day.

In Hebrew culture at the time of Jesus, reverence for particular teachers caused their students to argue their favorite teacher's point of view and to copy their teacher's ways. The students were called *disciples* because they were in daily fellowship with their teachers, *doing* what their teachers instructed. They learned their teachers' ways by literally serving them. The disciples of rabbis provided meals, ran errands, and made arrangements as they were directed. Gospel accounts describe the Twelve Disciples doing these things on numerous occasions.

Jesus was a teacher in this circumstance when He said, "A disciple is not above his teacher, but everyone who is perfectly trained will be like his teacher" (Luke 6:40 NKJV). In this, He told of the destiny of a disciple—a student being trained to become like his teacher.

If you are a Christian parent and are serious about child-rearing, then as you teach your child the right way to go, you are becoming a Bible teacher. From your young child's perspective, you have the standing and authority of a rabbi in your home. If he is a student living in the home with you, he is your disciple. As he approaches maturity, you are the image he is seeing and judging. For better or worse, you are who he is becoming. This unsettling thought might pose a question: do I want my child to be like me?

Becoming like the teacher is largely the effect of the relationship. Close, regular association offers the opportunity for modeling. In a home with children, breaks do not come often. If you have more than one child, the intersection of multiple crises can bring any moment to a boiling point quickly and unexpectedly. Under stress, it is easy to make mistakes in conversations or decisions while the children are watching and learning.

If you do not stay ahead of them in becoming Christlike yourself, someday you may see that they have become like their teacher in a way that you didn't intend. This is especially true about expressing emotions and controlling conversation under stress. Effectively modeling self-control over feelings is a critical teaching for your child because learning self-control is a classic characteristic of maturity.

The writer of Hebrews was thinking of this "strong meat" or solid food of instruction when he wrote, "Solid food is for the mature who, because of practice have their senses trained to discern good and evil" (Hebrews 5:14). Mature Christians are no less subject to things going terribly wrong than anyone else might be. But because of practice, they have "trained their senses." They continually monitor their inner life and are committed to persevering in peace. They are aware of the warning signals of rising emotions and show Christian maturity by practicing a deliberate awareness of virtues like vigilance, discernment, and self-control.

When you make a mistake in an emotional moment in front of your child, it can present an opportunity to teach how to recover. (As you know, he doesn't need any instruction in how to lose control and act badly.) If he is present in your moment of intense emotion—fear, anger, sorrow, or anxiety—he is watching and learning how to speak and act because he has those moments as well. If, in that moment, your emotions overrule your self-control, a simple, kind comment with reassurance that you will soon be okay is a great teaching for him. ("I'm sorry for the things I just said. I am really mad right now, but I'll be okay, and I love you, no matter what.")

The years fly, and one day, your child will be an adult in the next generation of family. He will have become like you. It is wiser to make allowance for this development than to deny it because the next step beyond not dealing with emotions effectively is *dysfunctional coping*.

We teach our little disciples only for a season. A disciple is a learner who is becoming like his teacher. Jesus said, "It is enough for the disciple that he become like his teacher" (Matthew 10:25).

We are their model.

Feeding Cats and the Power of God

In counseling, I often described how you feed a cat as an illustration for dealing with a child with a bad attitude. On one occasion, the mother on the receiving end was a committed Christian. She told me she wanted to use the power of God in her life, and she listened carefully. When I concluded the story, she said, "I believe what you said would work if I could maintain my self-control. But my child knows how to make me crazy, and I lose it." I had learned that I usually experienced anger in association with stressful situations. So I told a story from my own life.

Like her, I might feel anger in a moment of dealing with a stubborn child, but I had learned to keep my anger under fairly strict control. The policy and practice of apologizing when I *lost it* had led me to be less troubled by my anger spilling into my children's lives; usually then, the bad feeling dissipated. If there was a lingering tightness inside, I considered it to be a normal part of the stressful circumstance, not a spiritual issue. The feelings of anger were usually gone by the next day. But if the circumstance continued, the anger would likely return.

After my daughters left home, I was leading a Sunday discipleship class focused on love and Christian maturity. Preparing lessons that love "is not provoked" and that "the anger of man does not achieve the righteousness of God" (1 Corinthians 13:5 and James 1:20) led me to see that controlling the outward expressions of my anger only resulted in its suppression, not its end. This led me to confront my own need for the power of God. I had already learned that the power of God is released through confession and a determined commitment in repentance. Then one day in Haiti, the Lord showed me His power to bring an end to anger.

159

I trained for years with a medical disaster relief team, unaware that we were preparing for the day we learned of the earthquake at Port-au-Prince. News reports were increasingly alarming with tens of thousands of people dead and hundreds of thousands injured. When my team was called, there were no direct flights to Port-au-Prince. A flight to Santo Domingo and a dusty bus ride finally delivered us to the earthquake zone.

I was already winded when we arrived at the only building still standing. All around us were pancaked houses, collapsed walls, and crushed cars. Sparking utility lines flashed in the gray dust. The front porch of our barracks was unstable, and inside was a crowd of volunteers—engineers, well drillers, electricians, and medical people crammed in small rooms with too many double bunks.

At a refugee camp, I received an endless line of patients each day in the semidarkness of a little roofless church. The family of my Haitian interpreter was living on a blue UN tarp among the rocks of his yard. His sister was in Miami, having her legs amputated. I was glad to loosen my boots each evening.

I quickly fell into a routine in this crowded society of strangers. I kept my gear under the bunk, ate trail mix instead of the thick, spicy food served at supper, and showered during the time others were in the dining area for the evening meal. I also shaved in the bathroom in the early mornings before the others stirred.

Sleeping was fitful in the crowded quarters, and soon, I knew that I was about used up.

After several days, I was making my way into the dark of the bathroom and noticed an odor. With the light, I realized that some volunteer's undigested supper had been vomited over the floor, the sink, the tub, and the toilet.

I was experienced in third world medicine, and sometimes, dealing with a biological accident was part of the work. Without noticing any emotion in myself, I walked over to the two men who were coordinating all of the traffic and logistics in our quarters. They were quietly at work, the glow from their computer screens being the only light in the area.

"The bathroom's a mess," I said. "Is there a mop I can use to clean it up?"

"We know about it," came the casual reply. "The girl will take care of it."

I had seen "*the girl*," a young Haitian woman housekeeper on my way to the bathroom, doing her work. I *said* nothing. But I thought, *That's it? The girl will take care of it? The Haitians aren't suffering enough without having to clean up some American's mess?!*

It was dark and the supervisors could not see me as I felt a fury rising within. Before I betrayed my anger to them, I turned and began a search for a mop. I found the stuff I needed, returned to the bathroom, cleaned up the noxious remnants, and sprinkled extra bleach around.

I returned to my bunk to stew in my righteous wrath until dawn. In sunlight a little later, I was outside packing medicines when a white-haired lady approached and asked if I might be a doctor. Her husband had become sick last night and needed help.

My patient was in his late seventies, and as I suspected, he was the perp. He told me he was so stunned by the violence of his stomach's reaction to supper last night that he could only crawl to his bunk afterward. Cramps and vomiting had overwhelmed him, and now he was too weak to get out of bed. He hated to bother me.

I listened, asked some questions, and examined him. I told him he was dehydrated. "But the worst has passed. If you can sip fluids and hold them down during the day, I think you'll be okay."

He thanked me and asked if he could say a brief prayer for me before I left for the day. In that moment, I was again aware of the anger smoldering inside. On my way out, I found some oral fluids for him, spoke with his wife, and rejoined my team.

As our truck rocked across the ruins of Port-au-Prince, I felt the warmth of guilt creep across the back of my neck. Then I wiped away a tear. My anger was wrong, and if I didn't shake it, I would be compromised in the clinic work. In the dim light under the canvas cover of the army truck, I prayed, confessing that I was wrong and needed to be delivered from my anger.

Almost immediately, I felt the knot in my stomach and the tension in my shoulders melt away. My Father was with me. He had heard and intervened. No one but me knew about my anger. No one but me knew of the miracle I then experienced. And no one but me knew the lesson I learned: "If I surrender my body to be burned, but do not have love, it profits me nothing" (1 Corinthians 13:3).

As I finished the story, I told the young mother in counseling that her job was to love her son, not to fix him. Meanwhile, the divine spirit of gentleness inside her was there to relieve her anger. God would provide patience if she could believe the spirit of gentleness speaking quietly, "Relax—God's got this."

God can inject His power into our lives whenever He pleases. But He particularly wants us to ask for it so that we will appreciate it, and others can see its effect in us and glorify Him. When our expression of an inner virtue, such as patience, goes beyond our natural capacities, the reality of God's expression through us becomes visible to others, including, eventually, our children. Their transformation into maturity is a function of our own transformation.

We can do better.

The Parent as a Disciple

I befriended a young father when his wife was dying. I had met him and his little boy before he became a widower, but our first genuine conversation occurred when I made a home visit near the end of her life. On a subsequent contact, when I offered to be available to help his son work through grief, he mentioned that his child was now sleeping in the bed with him.

"That's common for a little guy who's just lost his mother," I replied quietly. "Are you okay with it?"

"I guess I am for now," he said. "But I don't want it to become a permanent habit."

Then he added, "Before my wife passed, she was primarily raising our son. I really don't know much about being a father."

I took this as an opening for me to give some advice. So I offered, "Your child sleeping with you is not a big deal and really not that difficult to straighten out if you decide you want to fix it."

He encouraged me to continue, so I spoke with him about how to gently and gradually wean his son back into his own bed when he thought the time was right. I told him that the retraining may require a few weeks.

He listened thoughtfully and said, "I understand what you're saying, but I don't have the patience."

I was reminded of the mother who asked me how to get her child to wash the dishes. I was also reminded of feeding cats. In that moment, a light shone on the greatest obstacle and the most critical confession of a realistic parent: "It's not about my child—it's about me." So I asked about his own experiences as a child and his relationship with his parents.

"My life was mostly spent playing outside my house. When my father was home, he growled a lot. I learned to just do as I was told in order to keep the peace. I liked going to church with my mother, and I learned some Bible. I didn't get in trouble until I left home."

He paused. "It's funny. I guess I got in trouble because I was finally out from under my father's threats." He continued, "When I became a husband, I earned a paycheck, but my home and my son were my wife's responsibility. She did a great job too."

He sighed. "Now it's up to me. I really want to be a good father, but I lose my patience and yell. I don't do well under pressure. Sometimes I'm in the ER with chest pain or stomach pain, and the tests are always negative. They say it's my nerves. When I'm too anxious at home, I get mad at my boy."

"What's making you anxious?"

"I don't know how to be a good father. I don't know what to do."

"Do you love your little boy?"

"Of course, I love him. I tell him so every day. When I'm not missing his mother, I'm thinking about him and how I want to be with him and what he needs and how to provide for him."

"When you were young, did you know that your father loved you?"

"I guess he loved me. He probably would have said he did. I know I was afraid of him."

"If he had told you every day that he loved you, would you have been sure?"

"I would have still been afraid, but it might have helped."

We kept meeting and talking; weeks turned into months. My friend was obviously emerging from his grief after a while, and our conversation became freer, beyond counseling. It became the talk of two friends. I began telling him stories about washing dishes and feeding cats. But mostly I spoke of God as our Father, the perfect parent who loves us far beyond where our imagination can take us. Since He is God, He is the one who initiates His love and determines its expression.

The Father exists in eternity with His perfect Son, whose excellence matches His own. But our Father desires more children to join His family. Among these adopted children are you and me, imperfect and challenging. Tremendous sacrifice by the Father is required to straighten us out and bring us to maturity.

God must have been thinking of that sacrifice from the beginning when "darkness was over the surface of the deep, and the Spirit of God was moving over the surface of the water" (Genesis 1:2). In this passage, *moving* translates a Hebrew word for *becoming soft or relaxed*, like a bird settling down in a nest with young ones. It is the word for *hovers* in Moses's narrative concerning God in the desert with His child, Israel. "He encircled him, He cared for him as the pupil of His eye. Like an eagle that stirs up its nest, that hovers over its young, He spread His wings and caught them" (Deuteronomy 32:10–11).

The love of God for His children is unconditional, flawless, fully committed, and everlasting. Love is more than a virtue of God's character; it is His very essence. It is entirely voluntary and cannot be earned. It continues even if it is unrecognized, unacknowledged, or unappreciated.

His love is a restless sea that seems always on the verge of spilling over everywhere. Yet it doesn't because it is limited by His holy righteousness. Meanwhile, our appreciation of His love is limited by our peculiar boundaries like ignorance, selfishness, and the uncomfortable sense that we are unworthy. If we work with Him and let Him build us up—like children being reared by a father who knows best—change and maturity are not only possible but exhilarating. The "beloved disciple" wrote, "See how great a love the Father has bestowed on us, that we would be called children of God" (1 John 3:1).

I told my friend, "My own father may not have told me of his love, but he taught me to listen and forgave me when I failed. Then, without my knowledge and without ever mentioning it, he endured the terror of war to pay for my education. Years later, in maturity, I appreciate what he did and am confident that he did it because he loved me.

"The Lord knows about your impatience and knows how to fix it too. He is in you, with all the insight and virtues you need to be the father you want to be."

Our conversation continued for weeks, then months. As he told me his story, I also spoke of mine. I spoke of my own confession and repentance and finding the power of God. Eventually, he moved beyond his grief and confirmed his purpose to be a good father.

Supplying Virtues

B abies are stewing in a brew of their mother's chemicals when they are born. Prominent among these hormones is oxytocin, the chemical that compels bonding. As the excitement of birth subsides and effective nursing is established, the peace of the two newly acquainted individuals is further enhanced by serotonin, a hormone associated with the pleasant sensation of tranquility. The brand-new, chemically enhanced relationship is intoxicating and critical to ultimate success in child-rearing. The sensations are the natural feelings of love.

The bond is strengthened through the years by a continuing conversation. Each moment of communication picks up from where the last one ended. As the teaching, practices, and learning go on and on in the comforting spices of love, somehow the things that are most important to the parent are transferred to the child.

When the child is not teachable, the resulting silence of isolation brings on the alarming chemicals of stress. Memories of the relationship bring the prodigal to his senses and call him out of the pigpen. A hope for forgiveness is a real possibility because of the long history of cherishing acceptance. With a contrite spirit, full forgiveness, and a renewed determination to cooperate, the conversation resumes.

So the love potion begins percolating again, and the things that are most important to the parent are again transferred to the child. This is how it is between parents and their children; it is also how it is between your heavenly Father and you.

Old Testament theology illuminates the path to love by emphasizing *not sinning*, expressed in the phrase, "Thou shalt not..." Paul recognized that love is contaminated by selfishness, so when he defined love, he included negatives as well (1 Corinthians 13:4–8a). He summarized the Old Testament law with a single negative, "Love does no wrong to a neighbor; therefore, love is the fulfillment of the law" (Romans 13:1) and concluded with "Love never fails" (1 Corinthians 13:8).

But Jesus has effectively dealt with the problem of sin for Christian believers, so the emphasis of the New Testament is more on personal sanctification and the practice of virtues. Virtues are morally excellent qualities of character manifested in conversation and behavior. Practicing virtues makes it possible for us to express our ideals of love more consistently.

The New Testament definition of love includes the positive virtue of patience. The Greek word translated as "patience" describes the virtue of bearing up in a stressful relationship or *enduring the unendurable person.*

The problem with unendurable people is that they can suddenly make you crazy, and you may just lose it. An example of such an individual might be a two-year-old who needs a nap. If you can somehow hang on to your patience with such a person, let's add a circumstance: he's bored and hungry, and you are stuck in traffic with him.

The need for patience is recognized by most parents, but patience is a virtue that is actually achieved through a number of other virtues. A failure in any one of these supporting virtues can begin the cascade called "losing your patience." For example, the virtue that keeps you from going crazy is *clear mindedness.* This virtue is associated with calm, sensible decision-making. In the Bible, a Greek word that represents this virtue is in Peter's first letter: "Be of sober spirit, be on the alert" (1 Peter 5:8).

Sobriety is associated with refraining from intoxication by substances such as alcohol and drugs; this is the clear meaning in certain Bible verses as well. But in this particular passage, being of "sober spirit" refers to resisting the influence of the intoxicating, naturally released chemicals that make us *feel* angry and upset. The solution is deliberately setting your mind with the virtue of sobriety.

Continuing with the passage, Peter directs not only that we "be of sober spirit" but that we "be alert." Being alert leads to considering *vigilance*, another supporting virtue of patience. The Greek word often translated as *watch* in the Bible literally means *stay awake*. Remember that clown with a pie is standing just beyond that open door over there.

With your child nearby, there is a selection of cream pies at hand, and you know the flavor of most of them. You also know where and when you will likely encounter them. With vigilance you can anticipate a pie in the face, avoid a mess, and maintain your patience.

A great principle of our Christian faith is that salvation is more than a ticket to heaven. It is actually a package deal that includes the divine person living inside us. Peter wrote that by the power of Christ in us, we have been granted "everything pertaining to life and godliness" and have "His precious and magnificent promises" to "become partakers of the divine nature." He continued that, since we have this faith that Christ is in us, His virtue or "moral excellence" is available to us: "Now for this very reason also, applying all diligence, in your faith supply moral excellence" (2 Peter 1:3–5).

We are invited to take full advantage of the Lord's presence and power as we deal with our children: "Take My yoke upon you and learn from Me," Jesus said, "for I am gentle and humble in heart, and you will find rest for your souls" (Matthew 11:29). Because Jesus is "humble in heart," He lowers His status relative to you so as to serve your needs. In His gentleness, He restrains the use of His authority so as not to be threatening or harsh as you work together within the yoke. These spiritual resources are yours and are a practical help through the regular meditation, prayer, and devotional life we all know is recommended in the New Testament.

Parents can feel isolated in their daily struggles, but the stress of this isolation has a solution. Surely our clueless and undisciplined children contribute their share to the struggle. But then we contribute our own share when we *lose it*. Cultivating patience begins by humbly confessing to our divine roommate our impatience and asking for His patience and power.

The Holy Spirit is like a gentle grandparent I knew who spoke of a conversation with a darling little terrorist visiting her home.

"Why don't you want to listen to me?" asked Grammy.

He replied miserably, "I don't listen because I can't *want* to listen."

So Grammy said, "I can help you with that. Just go to your room, and when you *can* want to listen, come back, and tell me."

She got it! And then, so did the child. "We are no longer to be children…we are to grow up in all aspects into Him who is the head, even Christ" (Ephesians 4:14–15).

The Mystery of Feeding a Cat

Perhaps you recall that I began this book by telling a story of a mother whose eleven-year-old wouldn't wash the dishes. Now, I'll finish the story.

On that office visit, after going through the necessary components of child-rearing that would contribute to a child's actually washing the dishes correctly when told, the office nurse peeked in the examining room and told the mother that she had a phone call she could pick up at the front desk. My patient and I were momentarily left alone together in the exam room, so I turned to the miscreant and asked, "What do you think of what I just told your mom?"

He pondered for a moment, a dark cloud across his face. "That would work," he said. Then the sun broke through. He brightened up with a smile and added, "She won't do it."

His answer caused me to recall the moment when I was first struck by the question of Christ: "Is this not the reason you are mistaken, that you do not understand the Scriptures nor the power of God?" (Mark 12:24). When child-rearing doesn't work, the usual reason is that flawed parents who are raising flawed children fail to fully apply the wisdom of scripture and the power of God. So, as Peter wrote, "supplying all diligence" in my faith, I am grimly determined now to finish telling you how you feed a cat by directing your unwilling child to feed the cat.

The situation was tense in my kitchen when I intervened in the dispute between eleven-year-old Julie and her mother about how you feed a cat. I had just undone all of Julie's poisonous efforts with the cat bowl and the closet door and spoken directly to her. "Julie, that's not how you feed cats." What happened next is the rest of the story.

Julie sat at the counter with the magazine prominently shielding her face, her mother continued to wash the dishes, and the cat continued to restlessly complain. I sat in stony silence.

Then Julie did what I trained her to do when she was a two-year-old with a bad attitude. On her own, she silently stood up and walked away to her room. Of course, she also added her final position statement by slamming the bedroom door. So here we go.

Several hours passed. The dishes were done, I was still reading a book, and the cat was still meowing. I heard Julie approaching from the pigpen. She plopped down beside me and read to me a poem she wrote. I'm sure it was worthy of Wordsworth, but it held no mention of her failure or of a change in her heart, so I browsed my book as she read her rhyme. She finished, looked up at me with a skeptical glint, and commented, "You didn't even listen."

"No," I replied. "I guess I didn't."

She produced a disdainful "Harrumph!" Then, she whirled away and concluded this first attempt at a peace talk with a door slam. About a half hour later, she returned, and things were dramatically different. She was in tears, and I held her close. She confessed, and it was over.

When we were okay again, I gently said, "The cat's very hungry. Let's go feed the cat."

We returned to the kitchen, where she quietly filled the cat bowl and put away the bag. She did it promptly, efficiently, cheerfully, and when first directed. (*That's* obedience.)

"That's good, dear," I said as I retrieved the bag, poured the food back into it, and returned the empty bowl to the floor and the bag to the closet. "You did that exactly right. Now please feed the cat again."

So she quickly refilled the bowl and put the bag away. (I could tell that because of practice, she was getting more skilled at feeding the cat.)

So I undid it all again. At this point, the cat was the only one who seemed upset. Julie and I were okay. "Please do it again," I said. And she did, and we were still okay.

And that's how you feed a cat.

It's also how you create a moment that becomes an indelible, pleasant memory, as it has for both of us. The genuine sincerity of our reconciliation was proven by her repeatedly feeding the cat promptly, efficiently, and cheerfully. The final proof that the lesson was learned was that we never again had a problem when it was time for Julie—not me—to feed the cat.

This moment of transparency in our relationship is worth another moment of examination. The reconciliation of the prodigal son required faith of both the lost son and of the father. The son would have to believe that forgiveness was a realistic hope, and the father would have to believe in his judgment that the son was truly repentant.

By recalling her history with me, Julie knew for sure that she was forgiven. She only had to be contrite and ask for confirmation. This had been her consistent experience with me over the years. She also knew that with a contrite spirit, she would always be fully forgiven and accepted.

As for me, all I had to do was to practice the virtues of patience until it was over. I would make no disparaging or harsh comments but rather simply be relieved and glad that she had returned. Both of us knew that our reconciliation was validated because we could both bask in that wonderful feeling of serenity.

David wrote of this moment in one of his shortest psalms: "O Lord, my heart is not proud, nor my eyes haughty; nor do I involve myself in great matters, or in things too difficult for me. Surely I have composed and quieted my soul…my soul is like a weaned child within me" (Psalm 131:1–2).

For both of us, it was not a moment of coercion, conniving, and obnoxious lectures, but of humility and gentleness. Humility is a deliberate, conscious lowering of status in order to truly be of service to another. Gentleness is restraining the power to overwhelm in a relationship and being as ready to receive as to give. In humility and gentleness, that magical teachable moment appears and actual *listening* is possible. As long as the relationship can be preserved in this state, the teaching can go on and on. Perhaps, forever, as far as I know.

The End; Also, the Beginning

Julie was in her last semester of high school when she faced her final exam on how you feed a cat. She and two good buddies were anticipating spring break and began considering the possibility of spending the holiday at Myrtle Beach.

I didn't know about Myrtle Beach when I was a senior in high school, but I did remember a few days and nights there as a college student. I was sure that high school girls looking for fun would be at a disadvantage on a long weekend because of older guys who would also be there.

As the girls effervesced in conversation, I practiced reticence and sobriety. I knew that within a matter of months, Julie would be planning weekends with her future college friends just as I had done thirty years earlier. My parents had played no role in my decisions at that time, and it was unlikely that she would be consulting with me about her decisions next year.

I was confident that I had won Julie's respect at this point in our relationship and that I had a reputation with her for doing what I said I would do. I also had confidence in Julie's good judgment and standards. I silently asked for the Lord's help as the conversation developed.

The three girls didn't seem to mind that I was in the room as they anticipated the sunny days at the beach and spoke of arrangements to make. When they had unwound a little and there was a moment, I interjected, "Julie, may I tell you something?"

I had their attention. "I was at Myrtle Beach as a cadet, and I remember high school girls being there too. I just want you to know that if I get a police call at two o'clock in the morning, I am not driving to Myrtle Beach at that time of night, and you will have to pay the legal costs."

Silence. I excused myself.

They decided they would go to the beach only for a day and return by evening. I never asked why.

The next year, I sent her off to college with high and realistic hopes that she would thrive and succeed. My hope was proven true. A few years later, my newest college graduate was using her education in modern languages as my interpreter in an Amazonian clinic.

Eventually, Julie became the hardworking, loving, and very effective mother of three children. I spoke with her about some of the sketchy moments of her childhood and asked if she remembered the times she spent in her room, accompanied only by her bad attitude. Oh, she remembered!

"You were really mad," I speculated. "I guess you were mad at me."

She seemed surprised at my question and answered, "No, I wasn't mad at you. I was mad at me. I didn't know why I was contrary. I knew I needed help, and you were trying to help."

"You knew that?" I asked. "How did you know?"

"Well, when I was sorry, you always received me back. We would always talk it out, and you would tell me that we will get past this someday."

Julie knew about me what the prodigal knew about his father. Our heavenly Father always welcomes us back when we are sorry. He doesn't use that golden moment for lectures or drama. He just wants to enjoy us again.

Among all of those whom God has loved through the ages, those of us whom He has chosen as His adopted children are particularly aware of His love. His love for us is at least part of the explanation for why He has revealed to us that we are the teachers of our children. It is also why He has blessed us with children who are dependent on us and compelled to bond with us.

In Scripture, He kindly gives us an understanding of two inherent obstacles we must overcome as teachers. The first obstacle is the truth that our children are only variably teachable; like us, they are immature and lack discipline. Like us, they are inclined to go their own way.

The second obstacle arises from the truth that we are compromised as their teachers because we have flaws in our character and lack insight. We resist acknowledging our flaws and only gain insight irregularly and apply it inconsistently.

Because of the Father's love for us, He has provided solutions for the problems we face if we will take them. He has given us authority over our children, along with wisdom and power for the best use of that authority. He has also given us a realistic hope for success if we call on Him for help and follow His lead.

Our heavenly Father is our great teacher. He knows all about us and our children. He created us the way we are and can make things happen when we don't interfere. It is our own childlike willfulness and selfishness, along with our ignorance and unbelief, that interferes. The Holy Spirit lives within us, informing us and empowering us as parents. By our faith and prayers, He also works with the hearts of our children to align their attitudes and bring them to maturity.

By God's provision, we are provided the curriculum for our children, as well as the method of teaching. The curriculum is called "wisdom," and the method of teaching is called "discipline."

By the wisdom of God, we can see an order for child-rearing. We cannot expect the child to keep his elbows off the dinner table if we have not first taught him self-control. We cannot expect him to learn self-control if we have not first established effective communication so that we understand what he intends, and he understands what we intend.

We cannot reasonably expect him to listen to us if we have not first taught him to regularly comply with our authority promptly, efficiently, cheerfully, and the first time we speak an instruction. And we cannot have this authority if we have not invested the sacrificial love required for him to be convinced that we only, always, want what is best for him.

Discipline—practicing doing it right—is experienced in the context of the bond which is initiated and maintained by the parent.

In this bond of fellowship, the teaching is *discipleship teaching*—the teaching is in fellowship and the learning is by doing.

Preserving the bond is the key to effective teaching. Because the child is inconsistently teachable and often makes mistakes, the first lessons the child must learn (by practicing) are to listen and to repent as necessary.

We have a high obligation to our children to remain ahead of them in maturity. Just as they are learning, we must also continue to learn. We have no control over the final outcome for our children, but we do influence their self-esteem and self-control. Meanwhile, the one thing we really can control is our own confession and repentance.

Through supervised practices, our children learn to walk alongside us on the path of wisdom, the right way to go. Meanwhile, we are also learning wisdom and so we remain on the right path. Together, we can enjoy each other because issues of *not listening* and *bad attitudes* are always taken seriously and resolved completely.

There is joy in child-rearing. It can be among the most satisfying experiences of life. "I have no greater joy than this, to hear of my children walking in the truth" (3 John 1:4).

Together on the Right Way

About the Author

Ed West is a retired baby doctor who has been studying how it goes between parents and children for a very long time. When he was a third-grader, he used to sit on his back porch steps after school and listen to loud voices coming from next door. Then the neighbors' back door would spring open and Earl, the sixth-grader who lived there, would suddenly appear terrified in midair, his legs churning and his remarkably disorganized hair exploding. Two steps behind him, his mother was also launching from their porch, strafing Earl with a broom.

Years later, Ed's education continued as a husband, a father, a pediatrician, a family counselor, and a Bible teacher. He has taught on the subject of biblical child rearing around the world and is still learning.

For Ed, the Bible is the authentic child-rearing manual, and its wisdom is the best hope for parents. He believes that parents are teachers and that they have to stay ahead of their children in reaching maturity. This means they have to change if they want their children to change. It's for sure that being a father changed Ed's life.

Ed's parents and his wife, Gwen, have helped make him who he was; the Lord is making him who he is becoming. Daughter Alice died of cancer before she could make a final edit of this book. Daughter Julie and Ed still happily recall learning how you feed a cat together.

Printed in the USA
CPSIA information can be obtained
at www.ICGtesting.com
LVHW050053100224
771275LV00001B/67